PHIL BARNHART

C.S.S. Publishing Company
Lima, Ohio

Copyright   1985 by
The C.S.S. Publishing Company, Inc.
Lima, Ohio

5807/ISBN 0-89536-723-8   PRINTED IN U.S.A.

Table of Contents

Absent Mindedness

A brilliant professor was noted for his absentmindedness. One day, after stopping to talk to one of his students, he asked, "Which way was I going when I stopped to talk to you?" "That way," the student pointed. "Good," the professor said. "Then I've had lunch."

Academia

Sophia noticed that, except when he was digging, Henry appeared happiest while working with the professors. It was clear that Academia was his idol in the same sense that Homer was his god.

Irving Stone, *The Greek Treasure*, p. 172.

Accent

"Have you ever heard of Iowa?" a midwestern American tourist asked an Englishman.

"Er, yes, of course," replied the Englishman. "I once overheard it in the conversation of a tourist from Texas."

"Is that so? And what did a Texan have to say about Iowa?"

"He said he'd be ready in about an Iowa and fifteen minutes."

Acceptance

The second step is to accept the gift." By grace are you saved through faith, not of yourselves; it is the gift of God." If that seems old-fashioned, here is a quotation of a man who could hardly be called an evangelist of the sawdust trail, the late Paul Tillich. "In the midst of our futile attempts," he said, "to make ourselves worth, in our despair about the failure of these attempts, we are suddenly grasped by the certainty that we are forgiven, and the fire of love begins to burn. That is the greatest experience anyone

can have. It transforms everything."
J. Wallace Hamilton, *Still the Trumpet Sounds*, p. 151.

My wife Sharon has taught me more than anybody about acceptance. She's taught me that when you love someone, you love him as he is.

I disappointed a friend who said to me, "Barnhart, I don't understand you."
I replied, "Charlie, that's okay, but do you love me?"
He said, "Of course I love you."
That's acceptance.

Accomplishment

A psychology professor conducted an experiment to prove a point about work. He hired a man to hit a log with the reverse side of an ax. The man was told that he'd be paid twice the amount he normally made. The fellow lasted half a day. He gave it up, explaining, "I have to see the chips fly."

Action

There is a beautiful little prayer chorus we often sing, "Spirit of the living God, fall afresh on me." In the original version of that chorus, the middle line ran thus — "Melt me, break me, mold me, fill me." Then someone with spiritual insight saw there was something lacking in the chorus and changed that line to read, "Melt me, mold me, fill me, *use* me." He was right. The filling is not an end in itself, but only the means of action.
John T. Seamands, *On Tiptoe With Joy!* p. 99.

Life is a short day but it is a working day. Activity may lead to evil but inactivity cannot lead to good.
Hannah Moore

The Holy Spirit is like electricity. He never goes in where he can't come out.
E. Stanley Jones

King (Martin Luther King, Jr.) was on the platform. I watched him closely from where I sat in a front row. He exhorted us to action, "It's better to go through life with a scarred body than with a scarred soul."
Malcolm Boyd, *Christian*, p. 164.

Adolescence

Adolescence is the age when boys discover the girls, and girls discover they've been discovered.

Adversity

Though such changes for a harder life may be "good" for people, it still depends on the people.
James Agee, *Letters of James Agee to Father Flye*, p. 64.

The brightest crowns that are worn in heaven have been tried, smelted, polished, and glorified in the furnace of tribulation.
Edwin H. Chapin

I love the story of Jacob wrestling with the angel. Jacob went away limping but he went away with a new name.

Adversity is the diamond dust Heaven polishes its jewels with.
Robert Leighton

Advice

According to an anecdote quoted by Voltaire, a beggar on a city street was asking alms when a passerby said to him, "Aren't you ashamed to be begging when you could work?" With dignity, the beggar retorted, "Sir, I asked you for money, not advice."

As I look back on my life I know two things: Often the advice I didn't want I desperately needed and often I should have sought advice when I didn't.

Affirmation

I am a special child of God.

So special
God created me
as a unique person.
There's not another person like me in the whole world.
I am a special child of God.
So special
Jesus came to show
that God loves me.
Loves me as if I am the only person in the whole world.
I am a special child of God.
So special
The Holy Spirit walks
with me every day.
Walks with me everywhere in the whole world.
I am a special child of God.
Thank you God.
Thank you so much.
Phil Barnhart

I attended a retreat where a man testified, "I'm thirty-four and I just found out somebody loves me, Jesus Christ." I wanted to shout out, "Where, for Jesus' sake, has everybody been?"

Perhaps the most positive word in the English language and the most conducive to continued growth in love is "Yes." "Yes" is the best "defroster" of frozen symbols and ideas. A lover says "Yes" to people, "Yes" to differences. He realizes that all things and people have something to offer him, that all things are in all things.
Leo Buscaliga, *Love*, p. 151.

For all the promises of God find their Yes in him. That is why we utter the Amen through him, to the glory of God.
2 Corinthians 1:20

Age

Youth is a gift of nature but age is a work of art.

Two elderly men sat on a park bench playing chess. An equally

elderly woman came "streaking" by without a stitch of clothes on. One man asked the other, "What was that that just went by?"
"I don't know but whatever it was, it needed ironing."

As you get older, work seems a lot less fun, and fun seems a lot more work.

A lovely senior citizen from Georgia, Miss Ethel Wade, quoted this to me years ago:
My bifocals help me a lot,
My dentures fit me fine.
My bra gives me a great uplift,
But, oh how I miss my mind.

Agnosticism

Don't be an agnostic. Be something!
Robert Frost

Alienation

Since spending eight years as a ghetto pastor my prayer has been, "Lord, deliver us from this period of polarization, this age of alienation. Bring brotherhood, restore reconciliation and grant us the grace to give you the glory."

Ancestry

What do you do with a God so open he lists a seduced seducer, a harlot, and an adultress in the genealogy of the Lord himself?
Carlyle Marney, "The Nerve to Submit," p. 12.

Angels

Are there really angels
With blue and purple wings?
Are there really seraphim
And other shiny things?
The sky is full of lots of worlds!
How funny God would be

If nothing lived and moved on them
But people just like me.
Agnes Sanford, *Behold Your God,* p. 7.

Anger

One of Beethoven's most furiously energetic pieces of music, called "Rondo a Capriccio" is subtitled "Rage Over a Lost Penny." Truly, it sounds like nothing more than a musical tantrum. As you hear it, you can visualize a man stomping around like an angry comedian in one of those speeded-up silent films.

Beethoven was known for his violent temper and his temper tantrums. The story is that one day, while walking out on the street, he dropped a penny (with today's inflation, one would hardly bother to pick up a penny), but couldn't retrieve it and, so, had a tantrum right there on the street. When he got home, he realized how silly he'd been, sat down, and wrote this wild piece of music.

God, may we all use our anger as wisely and creatively.

A soft answer turns away wrath, but a harsh word stirs up anger.
Proverbs 15:1

A man is about as big as the things that make him angry.

Answers

But why do the answers to our needs seem so hidden? Why don't we find them more easily? We do not know. The potentiality of penicillin existed in the universe for centuries before it was discovered. In the meantime, millions died of infection. Why are God's answers so deeply buried? It has something to do with our growth in the world. It has something to do with our free will. It has something to do with the extent of our truly passionate concern and disciplined dedication to search and discovery.
Flora Slosson Wuellner, *Prayer and the Living Christ,* p. 67.

Anxiety

Anxiety is not only a pain which we must ask God to assuage

but also a weakness we must ask him to pardon for he's told us to take no care for tomorrow.
C. S. Lewis, *Letters to an American Lady,* p. 22.

Tenseness, a way of life for Pete, was becoming a way to death.
P. Brandt, *Two-Way Prayer,* p. 22.

I tried to say it this way in a sermon: "Anxiety causes too much itchin' and twitchin', too much screamin' and steamin'."

Argument

Many an argument is sound — merely sound.

Ascension

The next aspect of Jesus' prelude to power for the disciples was dramatic and decisive. He ascended into heaven. This is the confidence of the movement: the assurance of the Ascension. He left them alone, a very startling way to teach! He had told them about it previously, "It is expedient for you that I go away." (John 16:7) How could his leaving them, or us, ever be expedient? Look at it this way. He had to leave them in one dimension to return in a greater demonstration of power. He left as Jesus of Nazareth, resurrected and victorious; He returned as the Holy Spirit, indwelling and ubiquitous. Now he was to be unloosed on all the world. People would meet him not just in Galilee, or on the Mount of Olives, or in Jerusalem, but everywhere throughout the whole world.
Lloyd John Ogilvie, *Drumbeat of Love,* p. 19.

Assurance

Assurance was the issue. As a servant I had no assurance. As a son I had a measure of assurance so as to testify a childlike confidence and love. I was an altogether Christian (though young and immature indeed) who not only feared God and worked righteousness, but whose faith, as the ground of all, knew (though not without some relapse into sin and fear) myself to be saved from damnation, the bondage of sin and to possess forgiveness and reconciliation with God.

Robert G. Tuttle, *John Wesley, His Life and Theology*, p. 199.

Atheism

Much is being said now about the rise of a secular man who is abandoning his old beliefs as though they had betrayed him. But the old beliefs have not abandoned him. They lie deep in his mind like a buried dream and they come to light in unexpected moments to surprise him, It's a bit like the old story of the Russian girl who was brought up as an atheist. She had taken a government examination, and like all students, was worried about some of the answers she had given. One particular question in the exam had bothered her: "What is the inscription on the Sarmian Wall?" She had written the answer: "Religion is the opiate of the people." But she wasn't sure, so she walked the seven miles to the Sarmian Wall to check it and sure enough there it was: "Religion is the opiate of the people." Greatly relieved, she forgot her ideology, blessed herself and said, "Thank God! I had it right."

J. Wallace Hamilton, *Still the Trumpet Sounds*, p. 132.

Attitude

William James once said, "The greatest discovery of my generation is that human beings can alter their lives by altering their attitudes." The Bible certainly supports that, doesn't it?

Authority

He (Paul Tillich) had the rare capacity of being an authority without being authoritarian.

Rollo May, *Paulus*, p. 19.

Backsliding

Sign in front of church: "Backsliding begins when knee-bending stops."

Baptism

I'm helped to understand the deep meaning of baptism when I recall the words of a country music song: "They baptized Jessie Taylor in Cedar Creek last Sunday. Jesus gained a soul and Satan lost a good right arm. They all sang Hallelujah when Jessie's head went under because this time it went under for the Lord."

Beatitudes

On a tour to the Holy Land I met a lady whose name is "Beata." Her parents named her after the Beatitudes. Perhaps they knew she'd become the "blessed" person she is or, maybe, she just decided to live up to her name. At any rate, they named her right. God help us to all become "Beatas."

Beginning

I planted a tree today
In the park on Beverly Glen
And when it's big and strong
We will have known
And loved each other
A long, long time.

Merritt Malloy, *Things I Meant to Say to You When We Were Old*, p. 63.

Being

Our problem is not over doing but under being.
Kermit Long

Belief

There is no unbelief;
Whoever plants a seed beneath the sod
And waits to see it push away the clod,
He trusts in God.

Lizzie York Chase

Atheism is rather in the lip than in the heart of man.
Francis Bacon

Jesus said to him, "Have you believed because you have seen
me? Blessed are those who have not seen and yet believe."
John 20:29

While according to the polls only a small percentage of the
American people say they do not believe in God, three out of five
have little interest in worship or religious institutional life. In practical decision, most of the time most of them act the same way
whether or not God exists.
Martin E. Marty, *A Nation of Believers*, p. 14.

Benevolence

Yes, Pip dear boy, I've made a gentleman of you! It's me wot
has done it! I swore that time, sure as ever I earned a guinea, that
guinea should go to you. I swore afterwards, sure as ever I
spec'lated and got rich, you should get rich. I lived rough, that
you should live smooth. I worked hard that you should be above
work.
Charles Dickens, *Great Expectations*, p. 351.

Best

In the movie, *From Here to Eternity*, there's a conversation
between the sergeant and the cook.
Cook: I do my best.
Sergeant: Your best stinks.
There are times when some think my best stinks, but God
always thinks my best is good enough.

Bible

Minister: What's the first book of the Bible?
Third Grader: Preface.

The Apostle's Creed does not mention the Bible. Apparently,
in early times the scriptures were seen as a resource to nourish

faith and not as an object to believe in. The Bible is our guide, not our straitjacket.

Douglas E. Wingerer, *Beliefs,* p. 80.

Paul said something to Timothy which should be the goal of every Christian who has contact with children, whether as a parent, teacher, coach, or neighbor:

"From childhood you have been acquainted with the sacred writings which are able to instruct you for salvation through faith in Jesus Christ."

2 Timothy 3:15

Alexander the Great slept with a copy of Homer under his pillow. He was not attempting to learn Homer by osmosis but was paying tribute to the great book. We pay tribute to the Bible not by putting it under our pillows but by putting its truth in our hearts.

I am a man of one Book. My ground is the Bible. Yea, I am a Bible bigot. I follow it in all things, great and small.

John Wesley

So many spend much time defending the Bible (its literal inerrancy, its historical accuracy, etc.). The Bible does not need to be defended; it needs to be declared.

The parts of the Bible that trouble me most are not the ones I don't understand but the ones that I do understand.

Mark Twain

The Bible is the spectacles we put on to see what is already there.

John Calvin

A man who had no interest in old books ran into a friend who had a great interest in them. As they talked, he casually mentioned he'd just thrown out an old Bible that had been packed away in the attic of his ancestral home.

"Who printed it, do you know?" asked the book lover.

"Oh, somebody named Guten . . . something," recalled the man with great effort.

"Not Gutenberg?" gasped the book lover. "You idiot, you've

thrown away one of the first books ever printed. A copy sold recently for $400,000!"

The other man was unmoved. "My copy wouldn't have brought a dime."

"Why not?"

"Some fellow named Martin Luther had scribbled all over it."

Bitterness

Bitterness imprisons life; love releases it. Bitterness paralyzes life; love empowers it. Bitterness sours life; love sweetens it. Bitterness sickens life; love heals it. Bitterness blinds life; love anoints its eyes.

Harry Emerson Fosdick

Blindness

In the play *Butterflies Are Free*, Don Baker, who is blind, says: "There are none so blind as those who will not see."

Boredom

A traveler canceled his flight to California because he had already seen the movie.

If you are bored, you can be sure you are, also, boring.

Brevity

The Lord's Prayer has 56 words; Lincoln's Gettysburg address, 266; the Ten Commandments, 297; the Declaration of Independence, 300.

But a recent government report on the price of cabbage contains 26,911 words.

Brotherhood

How to live together has been a problem ever since Cain killed Abel.

Clovis Chappell, *In Parables,* p. 75.

The sit-ins never would have been necessary if Christians had been sitting down together in church and at Christ's table all these years.

Dallas Lee, *Cotton Patch Evidence*, p. 190.

You can't spell brothers without others.

Busy

When God wants a great servant, he calls a busy man.
Moses was busy with his flock at Horeb.
Gideon was busy threshing wheat by the winepress.
Saul was busy searching for lost animals.
David was busy looking for his father's sheep.
Elisha was busy plowing with his oxen.
Nehemiah was busy bearing the king's wine cup.
Amos was busy following the flock.
Peter and Andrew were busy casting a net.
James and John were busy mending their nets.
Matthew was busy collecting taxes.
Saul was busy persecuting the friends of Jesus.

Call

The call, then, is a recognition of need and a willingness to meet the need if it be within our power. The reason most men hear no call is that they are not within calling distance, have not given their wills wholly to God, nor preoccupied their minds with these things.

Helen Shoemaker, *I Stand at the Door*, p. 40.

Our deepest wish is that America will be like the young soldier in the Civil War who got sick on the battlefield and was taken to the hospital tent. Lying on a cot, he pleaded with the doctor, "Oh, doctor, don't tell me I'm not fit for duty. Don't tell me I can't go back. It's only a touch of the fever, Doc, and the sound of the bugle will make me well again." This is what the whole world is listening for — a lifting up of a great purpose, a clear and positive blast on the bugle of the living God.

J. Wallace Hamilton, *Still the Trumpet Sounds*, p. 33.

Capacity

One of life's greatest tragedies is a person with a ten-by-twelve capacity and a two-by-four soul.

Caring

A recent study of why churches are losing members revealed the key is failure of people to nurture and support one another. Those who were closely identified with a congregation felt cared about in warm human relationships there. Those who had become inactive had done so primarily because they lacked feelings of being cared about. It is in communities of mutual caring that the fullest possible liberation of spiritual potential takes place.
Howard Clinebell, *Growth Counselling,* p. 26.

Categories

There are two kinds of people in the world: those who divide the world up into two kinds of people and those who don't.
Robert Benchley

Occasionally during the course of the first hour a patient will ask, "What is my diagnosis?" in a strained voice, braced as if for a pronouncement from on high. This is a provoker for a Parent-Child transaction, which I bypass with a question such as, "Do you need a diagnosis?" or "What would a diagnosis do for you?" It is my belief that more people are hindered than helped by psychiatric diagnoses. Karl Menniger agrees: "Patients do not come to us to be plastered with a damning index tab. They come to be helped. People can recover from the symptoms of mental illness but they don't recover from labels."
Thomas Harris, *I'm O.K. — You're O.K.,* p. 28.

Celebration

Our church choir presented "Celebrate Life," an upbeat musical representation of the life of Jesus. The music jumps and dances in rhythms of crescendoing celebration. It makes you tap your foot and sway your body. It puts a grin on your face and makes sitting still impossible. When our choir sang the Resurrection number, "He *is* Alive!," the congregation erupted in movements and noises of joy. They believed it and sang it and danced it.

God gives us a great life in Jesus. Let's celebrate it!

Ceremony

Oh God, may our performance match our pronouncements, our resolutions become revolutions, our liturgy be filled with life, our polity possess power, and our structure be dominated by Your Spirit. Amen

Change

Change isn't so threatening when it is approached as growth. Death isn't so frightening when it is approached as rebirth.
Maxie Dunnam, *Dancing at My Funeral,* p. 104.

My daughter brought home a stray cat — a mangy stray cat with sore eyes and baggy skin. We took the cat in and cared for her in luxurious fashion. Two months later, I observed the cat — beautiful fur, bright eyes, full flesh.
Was it the same cat?

A church youth group built a float for the city's annual parade. The float depicted the crucifixion of Christ. But instead of a wooden cross, the young people had a huge golden cross with lots of beautiful flowers around it. When their pastor saw it, he remarked, "It's interesting that the beautiful scene you have here is so different from the old rugged cross Jesus actually died on." "That's true, Pastor," said a boy in the group, "but didn't you tell us that nothing Jesus touches ever stays the same?"

Character

Contrary to some opinions, character is not created in a crisis. It is only exhibited there.

Children

To see the skies
Through children's eyes
No clouds are there
And all is fair.
And who could quite explain the joys
Of little girls and little boys?
Joy that comes without our knowing
And fills our hearts to overflowing.
Guard them closely in your prayers
A special heritage is theirs.
In words of one from Galilee
Who took the children on his knee.
Like these my kingdom e're will be
Forbid them not to come to me.
David Ogletree

"Listen when your mom tells you not to do things," said a small fry. "It gives you all kinds of neat ideas."

Choice

One way to get behind the eight ball is to take the wrong cue.

Choose it and use it or lose it.

Christ

When I was a very young minister I felt something I wish I could feel again. I heard something I wish I could hear again. It was the sound of Sandaled Feet walking beside me.
Jess Moody, *A Drink at Joel's Place*, p. 86.

James Earl Jones played the life of Paul Robeson. He performed masterfully. Asked how he did so well, he replied, "Paul Robeson was standing just off stage."
We live life more significantly when we remember Christ is standing just off-stage.

The great Shakespeare scholar, Charles Lamb, was asked what he would do if Shakespeare walked into the room. He answered, "I would get up immediately and joyfully extend my hand but if Christ walked into the room, I would lay prostrate on the floor."

In the second half of his work, Bonhoeffer speaks of the history of doctrines concerning Christ. The familiar distinction made by modern liberalism — the historical Jesus versus the Christ of faith — is rejected by Bonhoeffer. There is only one historical Jesus Christ. In this Bonhoeffer follows the conclusion of Martin Kahler. The Logos, who is personal, who is incarnate in Jesus of Nazareth, is confronted through the historical scriptural narratives and is known in no other way or form. The history of Christology shows that the wrong question has been asked: how rather than who?

Dallas M. Roark, *Dietrich Bonhoeffer,* p. 48.

Augustine brought the worlds of Plato and Christ together. Thomas Aquinas brought the worlds of Aristotle and Christ together. Jerome brought Christ to the heart of the Latin language, and Luther built modern German around Him. Our Lord found expression through the poetry of Dante and Milton and Shakespeare, through the genius of daVinci and Rafael and Michelangelo. The printing press came into being to spread His Word. And Bach and Handel set the Word to music. Our Puritan forefathers came to these shores because of Him. Each generation has found within it those ethical and spiritual giants who have made of Christ a kinsman. He has not been a vague religious form merging with the shadows of the past. He has been a vigorous and exciting Companion of the present, inspiring men to grander thoughts and nobler deeds.

James Armstrong, *Gentlemen . . . Start Your Engines,* p. 24.

Christian

The bitterness remained. The prison chaplain, Captain Henry F. Gerecke, visited Goering between seven-thirty and seven forty-five on the evening of October 15.

"He seemed lower than other days," the chaplain noted, "which to me was not surprising in view of things to come . . .

I broke in to ask him once more about his complete surrender of heart and soul to his Savior. Again he claimed he was a Christian but couldn't accept the teachings of Christ. On yesterday's visit I refused him the Lord's Supper because he denied the divinity of Christ who instituted this Sacrament. He furthermore denied all fundamentals of the Christian church yet claimed he was a Christian because he never stepped out of the church."

Leonard Mosley, *The Reich Marshall,* p. 388.

There are three types of Christians. The doctrinal Christians are considered Christians because they accept the doctrinal teaching of Christianity. Another class is composed of those who are simply Christian by implication, who live in a Christian community and come under the general designation of the environment in which they live. The third class are applied Christians, who make practical application of the Christian faith in the life they live in their human relations.

It does not require very extensive observation to discover that so-called doctrinal Christianity does not fill the bill. During the Spanish Inquisition, the doctrines of the Christians of that day led to the most gruesome and inhuman cruelty. The Protestant Reformation originated in doctrinal controversy, and cruel wars were carried on in defense of conflicting doctrines. Implied Christianity takes in a large field and a multitude of people. The community in which we live is spoken of as a Christian community because it has churches and social life that, in some measure, recognize and observe Christian sentiment. Applied Christianity is the Christianity of people who recognize Christian precepts and seriously and honestly endeavor to give expression of them in their daily life.

The true disciples of Jesus are those who keep his commandments. They are the people who conscientiously seek to practice the Golden Rule, to take thought of things honorable in the sight of all men, to love their neighbor as themselves, to keep themselves unspotted from the world, to avenge not themselves, and to walk humbly with the Lord their God.

"Sarasota Herald-Tribune," January 3, 1971.

The Christian, we conclude, is one in whom the Spirit of Christ is incarnate. By the power of the Spirit he participates in the life

of Christ, so that the presence of Christ and his Spirit has contemporary power and meaning in the arena of human relations.
Reuel Howe, *Herein Is Love,* p. 42.

He (C. S. Lewis) said somewhere that if the entire world became Christian, it would take very few years to make this earth into a paradise.
Evan K. Gibson, *C. S. Lewis, Spinner of Tales,* p. 39.

In hearing the phrase "small Christian college," I've wondered if that is a small college for Christians or a college for small Christians.

Christianity

Even those who renounce Christianity and attack it, in their inmost being still follow the Christian ideal, for hitherto neither their subtlety nor the ardor of their hearts has been able to create a higher ideal of man and of virtue than the ideal given by Christ of old.
Dostoevski

Christmas

If anything were too good to be true, Christmas would be. But if Christmas is not too good to be true, nothing can be. Dare to wish fervently and to entertain great expectations, for in a world where God reduces himself to infant size to make himself known to us, anything astonishingly good can happen. Christmas says it is so.

The business of the church is to help people understand and love Christmas. A woman was riding on a Milwaukee bus, when she noticed the slogan: "Put Christ Back Into Christmas Now!" "Gee," she sneered, "even the churches are sticking their noses into Christmas!" If the churches do not stick their noses, their minds, their hearts, and their wills into Christmas, there may be nothing left of the season worth saving.
G. Ray Jordan, *You Can Preach,* p. 155.

Clovis Chappell tells of a Christmas party he attended as a boy. It was in the village church and everyone was there. The tree stood bright with candles and loaded down with presents. Santa Claus pranced genially among the people, distributing presents to those whose names were called. There was a young feeble-minded man there, a hired hand on somebody's farm, looking at the tree with eager eyes. His name had not been called and his face was growing downcast when suddenly Santa Claus took down the largest box on the tree, looked at it, and called his name. A look of radiance came into the poor, stupid face as he reached out his hands for the box. With nervous fingers he untied the string and opened it; and then anticipation gave way to pitiful despair. The box was empty. Somebody had played a trick on the village idiot.

J. Wallace Hamilton, *Horns and Halos*, p. 17.

Church

Legend has it that, one time, in New York City, billboards suddenly appeared announcing that Jesus Christ would speak in the city on September 17 at 7:30 p.m. The billboard ads were joined by television, radio, and newspaper propaganda. On September 17 every church in New York was packed. But every one was packed with people who were strangers to one another. No one had attended his own church. No one thought Jesus would come there.

When the world looks at the church let's show the world a little bit of heaven.

In an historical view, the one evident outcome of the whole life and work of Jesus was the emergence of the Church, a society which regarded itself as carrying on the distinctive vocation of Israel as the "people of God," and yet was quite clear that it was a new Israel, constituted by a "new covenant." It had taken shape, not about a platform or a creed, but about a personal attachment to Jesus himself.

C. H. Dodd, *The Founder of Christianity*, p. 99.

We are not to be a religious memorial society of the past, but a vigorous movement in the present.

Lloyd John Ogilvie, *Drumbeat of Love,* p. 283.

My friend, Kermit Long, says that sometimes the Church is "Captured by a cash register culture."

C-H-U-R-C-H spells church only when U-R in it.

The metal is hot and moldable. Almost anything can be made of it. Perhaps not since the Renaissance has human destiny been so moldable. It is on the anvil now. For a few fleeting years it will be easily responsive to whatever will be made of it. Soon it again will harden. Then what has been made, has been made!

Hence, if the church has any redeeming pattern by which to shape it, a healing direction toward which to bend it, now is the time!

Everett W. Palmer, *The Glorious Imperative,* p. 17.

The Church is both an institution and a movement, both a conserver and a pioneer.

City

There are different ways of seeing the city. The statistician sees the city as a social unit, compressing so many parliamentary voters, so many Town Council wards, so many new housing sites, factories, industrial estates, art galleries, churches, schools. The poet sees the city as a fascinating silhouette against the sky. He stands in the dawn on Westminster bridge and cries:

"Earth has not anything to show more fair:

Dull would he be of soul who could not pass by a sight so touching in its majesty."

The moralist sees the city as a microcosm of humanity. In Sartor Resartus the philosopher sits in his high attic at midnight above the roar of crowded streets. Strange, he reflects, that all around me are those teeming thousands, men being born, men dying, laughing, cursing, hoping, fearing — "but I sit above it all; I am alone with the stars."

There are those different ways of "beholding the city." When Wordsworth saw the city, he grew lyrical over it. When Carlyle saw the city, he philosophized over it. When Jesus saw the city, he wept over it.

James S. Stewart, *The Wind of the Spirit,* p. 82.

Civil War

Better a thousand enemies outside the house than one inside.

What had happened to him was symptomatic of the times; and the story of the Lovells was the story of what was occurring up and down the eastern seaboard in 1775, with children turning against their parents, brother against brother, indicating that the war was going to be a bitter civil conflict as well as a revolt against the Crown.

Richard McKetchum, *Decisive Day: The Battle for Bunker Hill,* p. 197.

Claiming

And then the point of the Claiming Prayer becomes clear — the riches of grace must be claimed. "Ye have not because ye ask not," James cried. The process goes like this:

God has made a promise.

If there are conditions attached to it, we do our best to meet them.

We make an act of claiming this promise at a specific time and place.

God fulfills the promise in his own time and his own way.

Catherine Marshall, *Adventures in Prayer,* p. 87.

College

Two men were discussing their college student sons, both freshmen. The first man asked, "Is your boy going to be a doctor or a lawyer?"

"Right now," said the second, "I'm more concerned about whether he's going to be a sophomore."

Comeback

I watched again the movie, *The Monty Stratton Story* with

Jimmy Stewart. Stratton, a baseball player, has his leg amputated and attempts a comeback. After he pitched a game on his wooden leg I said to myself, "They amputated his leg but they couldn't amputate his spirit."

Commission

Not only those who proclaim Christ professionally are His witnesses, for Jesus says: "Go ye." That "ye" is all inclusive. It is a command, not a choice. It is an order, not an option.
H. S. Vigeveno, *Jesus the Revolutionary*, p. 197.

Commitment

My friend and colleague, Ben Johnson says there is no naked commitment to Jesus. "It's always embodied in my actions and talents."

I do not believe God wanted me to be in China for life, but I believe he wanted me to be willing to be in China for life.
Helen Shoemaker, *I Stand at the Door*, p. 25.

In the 1880s a bridge was built over the Mississippi River at St. Louis. Just before it was completed the chief engineer was called away on business. The foreman quickly discovered that the two ends of the bridge did not meet, being off a small fraction of an inch. He consulted the engineer who told him to wait for the scorching summer heat of the sun to loosen up the bridge material. That's what happened and when it did the foreman called the engineer again and asked, "What do I do now?" The engineer replied succinctly, "Clamp it!"

When God gets resources and opportunities ready for us may we make our commitment to his gifts. May we "clamp it!"

Years ago, a young man went to Paris to study with the famous piano teacher, Mme. Boulanger. She listened to him improvise on the piano and, after awhile, said to him, "I have nothing to teach you. Neither does anyone else. Go and start composing, Mr. George Gershwin."

There come many times in the Christian life when we know

God's given us what we need to serve and praise him. Those are the times to "start composing."

Rostov was silent; he lowered his weapon slightly, then he spoke, "Very well, a long time ago. What about now? No one's irreplacable, but you're a valuable man. Knowledgeable, productive."

"Value and productivity are generally associated with commitment. I don't have it anymore. Let's say I lost it."

Robert Ludlum, *The Parsifal Mosaic,* p. 24.

Dwight L. Moody once heard someone say, "The world has yet to see what God can do with one man who is completely surrendered to his will." Moody said, "I will be that man."

Committee

A city feller was hiking through the countryside when suddenly his attention was drawn to some odd goings-on in a field near the road. A farmer was plowing with one mule but he kept shouting, "Giddap, Billy! Giddap, Barney! Giddap, Moe!"

The puzzled observer hailed the farmer and asked, "Say, how many names does that mule have?"

"Only one," replied the farmer. "His name is Barney. But he doesn't know his own strength. So I put blinders on the rascal and yell three names at him, and he thinks two other mules are helping, and he does it all hisself."

That city feller thought that was pretty clever psychology and he kept thinking about it after he got back to the city. Now, if only you could use that kind of psychology to get a man to work real hard. Make him think he's got a whole lot of help. Just imagine how much he'd do by himself.

The next day that city feller went in to his office and invented the committee.

Common Sense

Common sense is the knack of seeing things as they are, and doing things as they ought to be done.

C. E. Stowe

Communication

The only thing some kids and their parents will ever communicate to one another is a head cold.

It occurs to me that thousands of men who hardly talk to their wives, children, or neighbors, buy CB radios so they can talk to some stranger in a car or semi two miles down the highway.

There is also an ancient tradition that the true lover cannot communicate the knowledge of the unity of things in any direct language. "Those who know don't tell; those who tell don't know." The enlightened man or woman coming back from nirvana has nothing to say.
Jim Fowler and Sam Keen, *Life Maps,* p. 122.

Could it be that one reason we have family gaps, generation gaps, cultural gaps, social gaps, economic gaps, societal gaps, and all other kinds of gaps, is that we no longer know how to communicate with one another?
So much so that in one suburban apartment complex they are teaching a course called "How to Talk With Your Neighbor."
Robert T. Young, *A Sprig of Hope,* p. 14.

Incarnation (exchanging one world for another), not just translation (exchanging one language for another) is the Christian model of communication.
John R. W. Stott, *Between Two Worlds,* p. 150.

Communion

The granddaughter of Sir Edward Burne-Jones tells in her reminiscences how her grandfather, the nineteenth century painter and stained glass designer, put one of his art windows depicting the Holy Grail above the sink where the scullery maid labored for hours each day.
A chalice above the sink. A communion cup beside the water tap.
Ernest J. Fielder and Benjamin Garrison, *The Sacraments,* p. 131.

32

The deplorable state of the prisoner grew worse during Holy Week, as a result of her being denied religious comfort. On Thursday, she suffered from not being admitted to the Lord's Supper; on that day, when Christ bids all to his table; when he invited the poor and the afflicted, she appeared to be forgotten.

Jules Michelet, *Joan of Arc,* p. 92.

Communism

If we Christians had more Christian communism, as the time of the apostles shows it to us, communicate sharing — "What is mine is yours; you are my brother!" — then we should not now have godless communism.

Emil Brunner, *I Believe in the Living God,* p. 45.

Community

Early in 1729, a serious man, Mr. Hoole, rector of Haxey, and my father's friend and nearest neighbor, said to me: "Sir, you wish to serve God and go to heaven? Remember that you cannot serve Him alone. You must therefore find companions or make them; the Bible knows nothing of solitary religion."

Robert G. Tuttle, Jr., *John Wesley, His Life and Theology,* p. 110.

Community, for the Christian, centers in Jesus Christ. This means three things: (1) A Christian is related to others because of Jesus Christ; (2) the path to others is through Jesus Christ; (3) the Christian is elected in Christ from eternity to eternity.

Dallas M. Roark, *Dietrich Bonhoeffer,* p. 62.

In team play, also, we see the occurrence of something that is very much a part of Christian character. In order for there to be team play, it is necessary for every member of the team to die to the desire in him to be the whole show.

Reuel L. Howe, *Herein Is Love,* p. 75.

We began to see into the ambiguity of our motives and those of our brothers and sisters and sometimes reached the limits of our capacity to understand, accept and forgive, or accept forgiveness. The "lowliness and meekness with patience, forbearing one another in love" (Ephesians 4:2) which we read about, was not easy to grasp. We found ourselves judging and being judged. It was hard to have to learn that the strong and the weak need each other, and harder to learn that each of us is both weak and strong. Through it all our egos were being pruned and our real selves began to emerge.

Robert A. Raines, *The Secular Congregation,* p. 76.

Compassion

There needs to be a revival of compassion, a deep, burning desire to win people. When Dwight L. Moody was in his prime he went to England to preach a series of meetings. A great preacher over there, R. W. Dale, was openly opposed to his coming because Moody was an "out and out evangelist." But Dale's people went to hear Moody. Finally, they began to come and say, "Dr. Dale, you have to come and hear this man. He is not like you think he is." And so one night Dr. Dale heard Dwight L. Moody. After that he went back night after night as long as Moody was in England. Someone asked, "Why did you go back when you, at first, were so opposed?" He said, "Because Dwight L. Moody could not talk about a lost soul without a tear in his eye."

Kermit L. Long, *Hungers of the Human Heart,* p. 50.

First, Jesus looked at the city. Then he wept over it. Then he died for it.

Henry Drummond

Conceit

Conceit is when you think you have some reason to have modesty.

Concern

The Savior is as concerned with a pebble that stands between us and a full free response to God as he is with a mountain.

Flora Slossen Wuellner, *Prayer and the Living Christ,* p. 80.

Confession

"Confess your faults one to another." (James 5:16) He who is alone with his sin is utterly alone. It may be that Christians, notwithstanding corporate worship, common prayer, and all their fellowship in service, may still be left to their loneliness.
Dietrich Bonhoeffer, *Life Together*, p. 110.

But we must admit the negative behavior to God and forgive ourselves, knowing that God will forgive us also. "If we confess our sins, he is faithful and just to forgive us our sins and to cleanse us from all unrighteousness." (1 John 1:9) The word confess means "to agree with God concerning." And the word sin means "missing the mark." Thus we agree with God concerning the fact that there are areas in life where we have missed the mark.
P. Brandt, *Two-Way Prayer*, p. 65.

In the play, "Same Time, Next Year" George is engaged in an extra-marital liaison with Doris as she, a Roman Catholic, speaks of confession.
George, worried, says, "You don't use actual names in confession, do you?"

Confidence

Once upon a time there was a man who was quite certain he was the most capable man alive. But, of course, he was not immortal and so he died. Just inside the pearly gates, he began organizing a choir, telling Saint Peter that he needed one thousand sopranos, one thousand altos, and one thousand tenors.
"What? No basses?" Saint Peter asked.
The man replied, "I'm going to sing bass."

Conformity

When all think alike, no one thinks much.
Walter Lippman

Conservative

If you want people to be conservative, give them something to conserve.

Consistency

Sometime ago, an army lieutenant won the national modern pentathlon title in San Antonio. At the end of the meet, he had scored the most points in horseback riding, swimming, cross country, pistol shooting, and fencing. But — get this — he did not win a single event.

Gerald Kennedy, *For Preachers and Other Sinners,* p. 19.

Contemplation

Festivity and contemplation are close cousins. The things that make life contemplative are the same things that make life celebrative — the capacity to step back from tasks and chores, the ability to "hang loose" from merely material goals, the readiness to relish an experience on its own terms.

Harvey Cox, *The Feast of Fools,* p. 123.

Controversy

Behold the turtle, it has been said. He makes progress only when he sticks his neck out.

Robert K. Hudnut, *Surprised by God,* p. 68.

Conversion

I don't know where I heard it but it's been a part of my spiritual counseling repertoire for twenty years or so. When a person faces the decision of accepting Jesus, I remind them that conversion is not a leap from one place to another; you simply turn around where you are and face a new direction, the direction which is Jesus.

In one of Peter Marshall's sermons there's the fascinating statement that "revolution comes through regeneration rather than regeneration through revolution."

Conversion is the threshold of religion, the front porch perhaps, better still the door into the central hall. Religion itself is everything one is and does in the company of God after he has

been introduced to him in this initial experience.
William R. Cannon, *Evangelism in a Contemporary Context*, p. 89.

My conversion thirty years ago started me on the journey of growth as I experienced salvation and moved into sanctification. I started as an amoeba and I am becoming a vertebrae.

I am walking evidence that the hell that is inside us can be turned into heaven.
Maxie Dunnam, *Dancing at My Funeral*, p. 3.

Counseling

In the last few years, I've quit trying to be a psychologist to people. In the first place, I'm not trained as a psychologist and have no desire to be trained as one. In the second place, I've concluded God has not called me to this kind of practice. He's called me to be a spiritual counselor, guiding people to a saving relationship in Jesus Christ and, after that, to the process of Christian growth. My tools are the Bible; prayer; the Holy Spirit gifts of wisdom, faith, discernment, and prophesy; all the fruits of the Holy Spirit; my own experience with Jesus and the experiences of others I can appropriate. While knowing that some people need psychological, and perhaps psychiatric, guidance, I believe my task as a pastor is to counsel people spiritually.

Courage

Courage is fear which has said its prayers.

In the musical, *Gypsy,* Rose sings, "Some people sit on their butts, have the dream but not the guts."

There was still time to do the courageous thing, but from moment to moment this became increasingly difficult and before he had given it any real thought, his inaction had turned into betrayal.
Herman Hesse, *Beneath the Wheel*, p. 98.

Creation

I forget who sings it but I love that song with the line: "Isn't she lovely? I can't believe what God has done, given life to one so lovely." But we can believe it. Just look at your family or gaze out the window. Or look in the mirror.

Why do you think I have given my life to creating a race of glorious creatures in marble and paint? Because I worship human nature as God's most divine attribute. (This is Michelangelo speaking.)
Irving Stone, *The Agony and the Ecstasy,* p. 679.

I've never understood those who pose a conflict between the opening chapters of Genesis and the deliberations of science. Science does not give us an account of origin, only of development. Even the notion of evolution presupposes something to "evolute" or change. It is not a theory of origins but of development. Whether true or not, it doesn't degrade God and his purposes for man.
Evertt L. Fullum, *Living the Lord's Prayer,* p. 62.

We are bold discoverers and ingenious creators, but we are not creators. We possess nothing that we have not been given.
Wallace Fisher, *Stand Fast in Faith,* p. 37.

Credit

Thoreau tells of the time he asked an old Irishman how many potatoes he could dig in a day. "Well," was the reply, "I don't keep any account. I just scratch away and let the day's work praise itself."

Critic

A critic is a person who would have you write it, sing it, play it, paint it, or carve it as he would — if he could.

Criticism

But, I said that I was saddened by one review. I didn't know

it, but later I was to receive much worse attacks, and would learn
to disregard them, at least partially, due to what Miss Pickford
said to me. She told me that in her entire career she never read
one review of her motion pictures. She said she thought that if
the reviews were good they might go to her head and if they were
bad they might discourage her. So her rule of thumb was whether
or not the public liked it. I asked how she could determine that.
She said the box office told her whether she was doing well or
not, not the reviewers.

Liberace, *Liberace: An Autobiography*, p. 37.

If you must criticize, criticize the fault, not the person.

I learned a long time ago the best thing to do when someone
throws mud on you is to let it dry and leave it alone; it'll fall off.
Don't rub it in or it'll be with you much longer.

Cross

The suffering of the event of the cross is not extraneous to God
himself. In the abandonment of the Son there seems to be an infinite separation between the Father and the Son and yet in this
separation the Father suffers the death of the Son. On the other
hand, there is an infinite unity between the Father and the Son
in their intention of salvation for us. As a result, we can speak
of a community of sacrifice between Father and Son. Reflecting
on God's suffering in the event of the cross will mean taking up
into the Trinity the full historical Godforsakenness of Jesus as well
as God's own suffering.

Jurgen Moltmann, *The Experiment Hope*, Forward, XVI.

The story Dickens tells in *A Tale of Two Cities* fascinates me.
Each night Sydney Carton made his way to his house to weep
on his bed over his wasted life. Yet at the end, he sacrificed himself
for the woman he had hopelessly loved by changing places in
prison with Darnay.

One life for another. Is this not what Jesus did for us?

A Christian architect was lecturing a seminary class on church
design. One of the students asked, "Would you put a cross on every

church?" The architect replied, "Maybe, maybe not. But whether or not I would put one on every church I'd certainly put one in every church."

The church with the Cross in it — the Cross on which God hangs for us.

While visiting Jerusalem and walking the Via Dolorosa, I learned that the original path Jesus took is buried six feet under the one I walked. It is difficult to understand all the mysteries of the Cross but they're worth digging for, aren't they?

A little boy, just learning arithmetic, went to church with his parents. He walked to the front of the sanctuary while his parents visited with friends and stood looking at the cross on the altar table. The service about to begin, his father came down the aisle to get his son. The little boy looked up at his father, back at the cross and said, "Look, Dad, there's God's plus sign."

Daily

In the movie, *The World According to Garp,* there's a line I've used on myself and it's helped me. Garp says, "You can live your life in one day and today I had a beautiful life."

Daring

I pray the word dare and its meaning will return quickly to the Church. To risk our ideas, talents, and energies is to be faithful to God's call and to the promise that, along with the call, comes the power.

Death

While in Jordan, an Arab told me about his friend who came to the United States. Reading the newspaper one day he was fascinated by the obituary column. Upon returning to Jordan he said, "There's the strangest thing about those Americans; they all die in alphabetical order."

Of course, we don't die in alphabetical order but we do die. Praise God for the opportunity to live abundantly before we die and, after we die, to live eternally.

"Parsifal didn't want you to be. You see, he never wanted it to happen again. No more Matthiases. Superstars are out. He never wanted you to be absolutely sure."

"I'll have to think about that, won't I?"

"It'd be a good idea."

"Matthias died this evening. It's why I tried to call you."

"He died a long time ago, Mr. President."

Robert Ludlum, *The Parsifal Mosaic*, p. 594.

Another patient's response may be, "Oh, doctor, how terrible; how long do I have to live?" The physician may then tell her how much has been achieved in recent years in terms of extending the life span of such patients, and about the possibility of additional surgery which has shown good results; he may tell her frankly that nobody knows how long she can live. I think it is the worst possible management of any patient, no matter how strong, to give him a concrete number of months or years. Since such information is wrong in any case, and exceptions in both directions are the rule, I see no reason why we even consider such information.

Elisabeth Kubler-Ross, *On Death and Dying*, p. 30.

The man who so envisioned the strange grace of God at work in his own life, his own region, the whole world, has now accepted as the final grace his own death. We have laid his body to rest with his father's in the cemetery behind the Salem Presbyterian Church, where he worshiped as a child. They came from all over the South to bury this man — from Richmond, from Atlanta, from Nashville, from all the very southern places, including Sumter County. Their faces were black and white. Many of them were distinguished people like the one they buried. But the distinction claimed by one of the mourners was what would have pleased James McBride Dabbs most: He was a mechanic who worked in a foundry in Greenville. He had been "stopping by to see Mr. Dabbs" off and on for thirty years. "Mr. Dabbs made you feel like somebody," he said at the funeral.

May the Lord bless and keep you, James McBride Dabbs. He blessed and kept us all a little better when he gave us you.

George M. Docherty, "The Christian Century," July 15, 1970, p. 869.

More than all the rest, I must say that for me my father (Sam Shoemaker) is very far from dead. His memory is crystal-clear in my mind, the things he said, the belly laugh, the twinkling eye, and sickness. But more than that, he is around every corner I turn. For everywhere I go I meet people, all sorts of people, endless numbers of them, it seems, that he has helped. They read his books; he led them to Christ; he got them into the ministry. How could a man be dead who helped so many? And, also, I find that as I wind my way forward in the Christian life, I turn more and more toward the way he did it. Eminently practical, this father of mine. It works, by gum, it works. It is contagious, and the same sort of religion he devoted his life to selling, and I never feel far from him because I want to sell it too. And so, in many ways for us, "death has no more dominion."

Helen Shoemaker, *I Stand By the Door,* p. 78.

Decision

But what is this surrender to God? It is more than an emotional lunge in his direction. Surrender is a deliberate, systematic decision to have done with everything in life which denies or disobeys God, and to take on his full will for us as far as we can learn it.

Samuel L. Shoemaker, *The Turning Point,* p. 12.

Resources do not limit decisions but decisions make resources. Do you remember Rosa Parks, a black woman, who refused to sit in the back of a Montgomery bus? She got into history not because of her resources, but because of her decision. That decision unleashed a wealth of resources from thousands of people.

Sometimes we need to think two or three decisions ahead so we won't be like the man who decided to catch a porcupine, and, after he'd caught the porcupine, had to decide what to do next.

Years ago two men emigrated from Scotland to Northern California. Each brought something which was meaningful from their homeland. One brought the seeds of the national symbol of Scotland, the thistle. The other brought honeybees. To this day, farmers battle the thistle and to this day, also, there are honeybees making honey in the mountains and in the forests. You can decide if you are going to plant thistles or breed honeybees. You can decide what you are going to do with your life.

Robert Schuller, *Reach Out for New Life*, p. 101.

We might withhold our decisions but we can't withhold our life. It gets made up.

Chess Lovern

Defeat

I often think of this with reference to the best loved character in American history. He was a young lawyer in Springfield, Illinois, who ran for the legislature and was defeated. Then he tried business and failed and spent many years paying the debts of a worthless partner. He fell passionately in love with the girl of his choice, and then she died. He was elected to Congress in 1846 and served one term, but was defeated when he ran for re-election. Next, he tried to get an appointment to the United States Land Office and failed. Then, as a candidate for the United States Senate he was defeated, and in 1856 as a candidate for the vice presidential nomination he was beaten again and when at last he became President, he faced the Civil War which he would have given his life to prevent. But in Washington today there is a memorial which I can never enter without having to force back the tears. Moreover, much as we deplore the hardships and troubles which Lincoln suffered, we know that his quality of character never could have come from ease, comfort, and pleasantness alone. He did not simply endure his tragedies; he built his character out of them.

Harry Emerson Fosdick, *Dear Mr. Brown*, p. 181.

Democracy

Channing Pollock, the historian, reminded us that most of the great democracies have lasted about two hundred years. He analyzed the historical cycle of democracies this way:

1. Mankind progresses from bondage to spiritual faith.
2. From spiritual faith to courage.
3. From courage to freedom.
4. From freedom to abundance.

5. From abundance to selfishness.
6. From selfishness to apathy.
7. From apathy to dependency.
8. From dependency to bondage.

Demonic

People often ask me if I believe in demons and I reply: "Only when I'm possessed by one."

Denominationalism

A friendly dispute over religion had gone on for years between two neighboring farmers, one a Quaker and the other a Baptist. The Quaker was confident that his way of living would earn him entry into heaven, but the Baptist constantly warned him that he would never make it without being baptized. Both reached advanced age without resolving the argument, and one day, while hobbling along inspecting their fences, they met. "Well, Matthew," said the Baptist, "I reckon neither one of us has much time left here on this earth, and as you've been a mighty fine neighbor, I'm really going to miss you up in heaven."

"I'll tell you what, Roy," said the old Quaker, "when thee gets up there, if thee should happen to see a right leg floating around, thee might greet it by my name. At a dinner once long ago, a Baptist minister spilled a glass of drinking water on my leg."

It occurs to me that denominational names are adjectives and not nouns; they modify the noun. The words Baptist, Roman Catholic, Presbyterian, even Non-Denominational, and so forth, are all adjectives. The noun is "Christian." We are Lutheran Christians, Methodist Christians, and so forth. Let us not substitute the adjective for the noun.

Depression

My friend, Carlyle Marney, said depression is having no "I."

Desire

God does not ask a perfect work but only infinite desire.
Saint Catherine of Siena

Despair

We use despair in order not to see things. We become very cynical and critical of any possibility of change in order to protect ourselves from seeing just where we are.

Robert Coles, *The Geography of Faith,* p. 59.

Details

In my hometown newspaper I read that the entire unique mass transit system at West Virginia University had been shut down. When the cause was discovered, it was a deficient three-eighth-inch nut that cost five cents.

Determination

Don't be a giver-upper,
Set your chin.
Don't be a giver-upper,
You can win.
When the going's rough and rugged,
Stick around.
Don't let the ship you're sailing
Run aground.
The motto of a winner's
Always been:
Don't be a giver-upper,
Try again.

I remember reading the results of the 1977 National Football League Draft in the newspaper: "Rob Lytle, running back, University of Michigan, six feet one, a player whose intensity enables him to be better than he should be."

Alexander White, an illegitimate child, was called to the ministry in his teens. He had no money but he worked hard and finally went to the University of Edinburgh. He and another student lived in virtual poverty. They had only one bed and would sleep six hours and study six hours, alternating in the bed. They worked part-time and used all of their money for books to equip themselves. This man was great because he was called and determined.

Detour

The longer I've lived the more I'm convinced that the best part of the day is often the interruption.

Devil

Whenever God erects a house of prayer
The devil always builds a chapel there;
And 'twill be found upon examination
The latter has the largest congregation.
Daniel Defoe

Dialectic

It occurs to me that in human relationships, the dialectic is when we hold someone with open arms — when we hold him and let him go at the same time.

Diet

A secretary lunching in a local restaurant noticed a friend at a nearby table. As she stopped to say hello she noticed her friend was nibbling at a cottage cheese-lettuce salad.
"Trying to lose weight?" she asked.
"No," the friend said, "I'm on a low salary diet."

Difficulty

The best way out of a difficulty is through it.

Difficulties are things that show what men are.
Epicletus

I used a cliche on a lady once who was having difficulty. I said, "a journey of a thousand miles begins beneath your feet."
She replied, "Yes, but I keep stubbing my toe."

Diplomacy

A high school student looked up from a textbook and asked his father, "Dad, what is meant by 'diplomatic phraseology'? "

"Well son," the father replied, "if you said to a homely girl, 'Your face would stop a clock,' that would be stupidity. But if you said to the same girl, 'When I look into your eyes, time stands still,' that would be diplomatic phraseology."

Discipline

For the moment all discipline seems painful rather than pleasant; later it yields the peaceful fruit of righteousness to those who have been trained by it.
Hebrews 12:11

In Greenwich Village I often see one young girl whose skirt is so short you wouldn't believe it. I know her father, a highly respected minister. One day this girl came to me with a strange confession. "My dad knows how I dress and the kind of friends I run around with. Sometimes I think he's going to bawl me out, but every time he chickens out. I can't handle it. He's too easygoing and I'm paying the price. Why doesn't my father try to do something to keep me from going to hell?"
David Wilkerson, *Hey, Preacher, You're Comin' Through,* p. 123.

Disturbance

We sing "Blessed assurance, Jesus is mine." Sometimes we need to sing, "Blessed disturbance when I realize I am His."

Doctrine

Happy a man deems himself should he discover a doctrine, even if not demonstrably true, which both takes account of the instinct and does not overstimulate it; which disentangles or states its meaning clearly, and in practice, guides and governs it.
C. C. Martindale, *God and the Supernatural,* p. 31.

Driving

How to make a left turn in Los Angeles: Follow the driver who turns left on the yellow light. The wreckage of his car will block the oncoming traffic until you can get through.

Drugs

Back then we had our bootleg hootch
To help us dissipate.
In rumble seats we'd booze and smooch
Our souls to vitiate.
Now it's with drugs the kids inflame
The freaking-out mishaps.
The kicks have changed, but it's the same
Degeneration gap.

Duty

There's the story of the careless mailman who decided to save some of the mail until a light day. The light day never came and, when he was discovered, he had in his possession ten thousand pieces of undelivered mail. Think of the lives this changed and the things it caused. We must deliver every day what we are supposed to deliver.

Easter

After every crucifixion there is a resurrection.
After every funeral, there is a festival.
After every sunset, there is a sunrise.
After every eclipse, there is an Easter.

Ecumenism

The true liberal spirit allows one to accept the fact that the Living Water can be carried in different vessels.
Harry Emerson Fosdick

No one form of church can be absolutized. This asserts a center other than Jesus.
Ralph Shotwell

Education

Now I sit me down to study.
I pray the Lord I don't go nutty;
And if I should fail to learn this junk,
I pray the Lord that I don't flunk.
So now I lay me down to rest
And I pray I'll pass tomorrow's test.
If I should die before I wake,
That's one less test I'll have to take.

Confucius was a learner all of his life and looked upon all men as his teachers.
Charles Francis Potter, *The Faiths Men Live By,* p. 82.

Effort

There is a great story from Herman Hesse who tells of Hans who is taking the state examination to get into the university. Hans comes in second in the whole country, his teacher gives him the news, and asks him how he feels about it. Hans replies that if he'd known he could have come in second, he would have come in first.
Herman Hesse, *Beneath the Wheel,* p. 31.

"Put on the whole armor of God." The verb rendered "put on" is an aorist middle (reflective) form, a command to do something within or for yourself. So, literally, it reads, "Get yourselves clothed with the panoply of God." God gives the armor. But each Christian must get himself clothed with it. He must put it on himself. The figure here is that of a Roman officer giving a soldier his armor which the soldier had to put on himself.
Herschel H. Hobbs, *New Men in Christ,* p. 119.

Ego

Egotist: a person who's me-deep in conversation.

Elderly

Blessed are they who understand
My faltering step and palsied hand.

Blessed are they who know that my ears today
  Must strain to catch the things they say.
Blessed are they who seem to know
  That my eyes are dim and my wits are slow.
Blessed are they who looked away
  When coffee spilled at the table today.
Blessed are they with a cheery smile
  Who stopped to chat for a little while.
Blessed are they who never say
  "You've told that story twice today."
Blessed are they who know the ways
  To bring back the memories of yesterdays.
Blessed are they who make it known
  That I am loved, respected, and not alone.
Ester Mary Walkers

Enemies

"Pray for your enemies," Jesus said. He said it because it is impossible. The minute you pray for an enemy, he is no longer an enemy, but a brother. The prayer is thrown over him like a cloak of relationship. The situation is altered, transmuted.

The enemy may not realize it immediately, but something has changed. We are not, for him at least, who we were. We have begun to see with new eyes. Soon other things must change too — things outside us, things between us, things in the world.

John Killinger, *Bread for the Wilderness, Wine for the Journey*, p. 71.

Envy

Sometimes the only reason people envy other people is that they don't know them very well.

When he first began soliciting subscriptions for the library, he met with "objections and reluctances" and swiftly saw that the trouble was the envy which others felt when a man presented himself as "the proposer of any useful project that might be supposed to raise one's reputation in the smallest degree above that of one's neighbors." From that moment, Franklin put himself, "as much as I could out of sight," and described the project as "a scheme of a number of friends" who had requested him to gather the support of "lovers of reading." The library was soon thriving, and Franklin applied this strategy with equal success in all the other public projects with which he became involved.

Thomas Fleming, *The Man Who Dared Lightning*, p. 17.

Esteem

Someone said Lyndon Johnson did not suffer from a bad education; he suffered from the belief that he had had a bad education.

Eternal Life

The truest end of life is to know that life never ends.
William Penn

Dr. F. B. Meyer, one of the great Christians of another generation, wrote to a friend a day or two before his death, "I have just heard, to my surprise, that I have only a few days to live. It may be that before this reaches you I shall have entered the Palace. Don't trouble to write. We shall meet in the morning. With much love, yours affectionately, F. B. Meyer."

When Michael Faraday, the great scientist, lay dying, a friend asked him, "What are your speculations?" Gently, Faraday replied, "Speculations? I have none. I rest my soul on certainties."

Over the arch doorways to the Cathedral of Milan are the three mottos —
On the left: "All that which pleases is but for the moment."
On the right: "All that troubles is but for the moment."
Central door: "That only is important which is eternal."

Clemson University economist Bruce Yandle collects graffiti for his own enjoyment and for use in his lectures. When Yandle is in the doldrums, his spirits are lifted by one of the first pieces of graffiti he collected. Beneath the question, "Where will you spend eternity?" A student had answered, "The way it looks now, in Economics 201."

Ethics

Warren Burger, Chief Justice of the Supreme Court, says "The biggest problem today is the corruption of the ethics of doctors and lawyers."

Eulogy

If any of you are around when I have met my day, I don't want a long funeral. Tell them not to mention that I have a Nobel Peace Prize. That isn't important. I'd like somebody to mention that I tried to love somebody. That I did try to feed the hungry, that I did try to clothe those who were naked.
Martin Luther King, Jr.

Evangelism

The church exists primarily for those who never go near it.
William Temple

Our Lord's parables often emphasize an actual finding. The woman does not merely search, but searches till she finds the lost coin. The shepherd does not make a token hunt and return empty-handed. He goes after the one which was lost until he finds it.
Donald McGavran, *Understanding Church Growth*, p. 41.

Evil

An Arab shiek came in from the desert with a pocketful of dates, held one up to a candle but it had a worm in it so he picked up the second one. Holding it up to the candle, he discovered it, too, had a worm. Three more, one at a time, held to candlelight each revealed a worm. So the shiek blew out the candle and ate all the dates.
The light of Jesus reveals the evil in our lives. Too often we remove the light rather than remove the evil.

52

Evolution

I stood before the monkey's cage
Their funny ways to see.
I laughed at them a lot until
I saw one laugh at me.
R. McCann

Excitement

I heard Bishop Roy Nichols preach in Macon, Georgia, several years ago when he told of his concern for his grandmother's faith. As a child he watched his grandmother sit quietly in church while others shouted and ran up and down the aisles. When he asked his grandmother if she really had religion, she answered, "It's not how high you jump but how straight you walk when you hit the ground that makes the difference."

Expectation

To live without expecting something is to be dead.
G. Ray Jordan

I presently pastor a church where I expect more from the laity than anywhere I've been. And I'm getting more. A lot more.

Experience

A minister was describing the power of God to change life and he asked the man in the front row:
"Do you believe this can happen?"
"Yes."
"Why?"
"Because it has happened to me."

A friend from Florida told me he'd shaken more sand out of his shorts than most people had walked over.

Don't separate experience and evangelism. If I've experienced Jesus I'll have something to say about him.

Expert

An expert is an ordinary person a long way from home.

Failure

The recognition of personal failure is the beginning of hope for a better life.
Robert T. Young, *A Sprig of Hope*, p. 33.

In the movie, *The Verdict*, Frank Galvin (portrayed by Paul Newman), a has-been lawyer on the comeback trail, considers giving up a seemingly impossible case. His girlfriend says to him, "If you want to be a failure, Frank, go somewhere else; I don't invest in failures."

Faith

Blaise Pascal developed his own reflections on this question. Pascal observed that there are three major sources of faith: custom, reason, and inspiration. By custom he means the witness we receive from the experience of other men and women, both contemporary and historical. The traditions and lives of people around us and of those who have lived before us affirm to our lives the credibility of the Christian gospel. Reason, as Pascal sees it, is the internal weighing and questioning of the truthfulness of it all, reasoning that we must do for ourselves, the kind of thing no one else should ever attempt to do for us. We, individually, must struggle to line up the affirmation of the Scripture and the church alongside our own doubts and fears and confusion and the credibility of all other possible options. Inspiration is the mysterious self-confirmation by which God himself is his own authentication. Here Pascal points to the ministry of the Holy Spirit which assures us of the authority, the reality, and the love of God's Speech — Jesus Christ.
Earl F. Palmer, *Love Has Its Reasons*, p. 73.

When we speak of the Christian faith, we often mean a body of doctrine. To be a Christian means to believe certain things. But faith is much more than belief; it is the experience of trust and commitment as well. "Belief" is the word we use to describe the meaning this experience has for us.

Douglas E. Wingerer, *Beliefs,* p. 29.

Basic to Paul's line of thought in Romans is his conviction, growing out of his personal experience, that salvation could not be had through the law. The law could not empower man to achieve it. Therefore God in sending Christ opened a way whereby through faith in him man is accepted on the basis, not of works, but of faith.

Charles M. Laymon, *They Dared to Speak for God,* p. 145.

Yet, what we expect need not be determined by outside circumstances, nor by what happens to us. Wasn't it a poet who said, "That which is beautiful in life comes from within?" When we look about us and see a John Milton, blind and yet able to write those lovely sonnets, then we can surely say that life need not be controlled by what happens to us. When we realize that Beethoven wrote some of his finest music after he had become deaf, how can we doubt that this is true? *Pilgrim's Progress,* whose sales in English have only been surpassed by the Bible itself, was written by a man in jail. The principal character in that story, a man by the name of "Christian," traveled through discouragement and against obstacles. Why? Because his mind and heart were focused upon that Celestial City which was the goal of his every effort. What happens to us surely affects us, but for a person who would faithfully commit his confidence to the personal God, it need not control what he expects from life.

Wilson O. Weldon, *Mark the Road,* p. 69.

For when faith says it "knows," it does not know what it is talking about. Even the Christ had to faith his way through death. Who would refuse to die for the sins of the world for three days if he knew he would rise? He faithed his way; he pulled no rank on us! He faithed that the purpose of God would bring him through, and the Christian faith hangs on what the Father did!

Carlyle Marney, *Faith in Conflict,* p. 151.

Oh, for trust that brings the triumph
When defeat seems strangely near;

Oh, for faith that changes fighting
Into victory's ringing cheer;
Faith triumphant
Knowing not defeat nor fear.

God does not die on the day when we cease to believe in a personal deity, but we die on the day our lives cease to be illumined by the steady radiance renewed daily, of a wonder, the source of which is beyond all reason.
Dag Hammarskjold, *Markings,* p. 56.

Family

And that was the atmosphere in which I grew up. I became determined to succeed in the material sense. Later I realized that material success is only one kind of success — the American kind, I hate to say. But if you have a mind and an education, some degree of culture, of literacy, of sensitivity, you discover early on that money is not the answer. You discover early on that there is a great deal more you want out of life. You discover that life is in your home, your family. And that's where I've been successful.
Howard Cosell, *Cosell,* p. 126.

In checking your family tree you might find some nuts.

But what on earth is half so dear
So longed for — as the hearth of home?
Emily Bronte

Fanaticism

Fanaticism is redoubling your efforts when you have forgotten your aim.
George Santayana

Father

In the play *Butterflies Are Free,* Don Baker says, "He's the kind of man who would have been my best friend even if he hadn't been my father."

A dear friend of mine, Tom Are, has a son in seminary who was speaking at his former college and said, "Some of you pious people here say you want to become like Jesus. That's too ambitious and lofty for me. I just want to be like my dad."

A father attending his son's Little League baseball game was pressed into umpiring third base, a duty for which he was unequipped. Adding insult to injury, his son played baseball poorly and, more insult, a heckler in the stands kept criticizing his umpiring. Through some miracle his son got a hit, rounded first, second, headed for third. He slid in, the third baseman tagged him, and he was out by a mile. "Safe!" his father cried. The heckler ran from the stands, onto the field, yelling, "That was awful! You're a terrible umpire." He replied, "You're right, but I'm one heck of a father."

Faults

A man was applying for the job of private secretary to Winston Churchill. Before introducing him, an aunt of Churchill's told the man: "Remember, you will see all of Winston's faults in the first five hours. It will take you a lifetime to discover all his virtues."

Fears

I hope your next letter will bring me news that the operation has gone swimmingly. Fear is horrid, but there's no reason to be ashamed of it. Our Lord was afraid (dreadfully so) in Gethsemane. I always cling to that as a comforting fact.
C. S. Lewis, *Letters to an American Lady*, p. 39.

Fellowship

So we must provide The Miracle or we have no justification for being. And no right to expect anyone to pay any attention to us. Let us deserve to be heard and we will be. What kind of miracle will cause the world to sit up and take notice? The miracle of a different and better fellowship.
Jess Moody, *A Drink at Joel's Place*, p. 18.

Flattery

Flattery is the art of telling a person exactly what he thinks of himself.

Following

When the early Christians went out into the Roman world they had no bulging briefcases full of programs and plans for changing the world. All they had was their lives, their witness, their unwavering loyalty to Christ. Before they were called Christians they were called Followers of the Way. That's what Jesus had called himself, "I am the way. Follow me." So it was immensely simplified for them. God had made his purpose clear for every life, not in a system or a philosophy to figure out nor an ethical code, but in a Person. Christ was the way and they followed him.
J. Wallace Hamilton, *Overwhelmed,* p. 18.

Forgetfulness

I wish I had a dollar
For each clever thing I've said
Once the party's over,
And I am home in bed.
Gertrude Pierson

Forgiveness

If there's a waste can in the kitchen filled with smelly garbage, you can move it to the corner and that might help. Or you can put it out on the porch and that'll help more. But what you really need is someone who'll come and take the smelly garbage away.
That's what God did in Jesus who forgives us.

Doing an injury puts you below your enemy; revenging one makes you even with him; forgiving it sets you above him.
Thomas Fleming, *The Man Who Dared the Lightning,* p. 409.

In the movie, *The Best Little Whorehouse in Texas,* Mona (portrayed by Dolly Parton) asks Ed Earl (portrayed by Burt Reynolds),

"How come God forgives me and people don't?" Ed Earl answers, "People aren't very godly."

Freedom

And that kind of living does not allow an unmastered life. This is why so many people today think they are going to have and enjoy an unmastered life. But there is no such thing. It is pyschologically impossible. Show me just one unmastered life — just one! I see people mastered by crazes, fads, passing fashions. I see people mastered by selfish ambition, driven like slaves to achieve their dreams of avarice or power. I see people mastered by habits — drink, drugs, temper, lust — in a tyranny they cannot disobey. I see people mastered by their own moods, tossed to and fro like rudderless boats. I see people mastered by fears — afraid of life, of death, of themselves, of tomorrow. And — thank God! — I see people mastered by unselfish devotion to their home, by the joy and pride of good workmanship, by love for their fellows and dedication to great causes. I see people mastered by Christ — the love of Christ constraining them, as Paul said — so that they walk through this world as though they were keeping step to music from far above it. That is being a real non-conformist. Freedom is not living an unmastered life — that is an impossibility. Freedom is being mastered by something that it is worthwhile being mastered by.

Harry Emerson Fosdick, *Dear Mr. Brown,* p. 147.

"Why is it," Jonathan puzzled, "that the hardest thing in the world is to convince a bird that he is free, and that he can prove it for himself if he'd just spend a little time practicing? Why should that be so hard?"

Richard Bach, *Jonathan Livingston Seagull,* p. 122.

Free Will

To ask that man should have been made so that he was not able to revolt is to ask that God's creation should have ceased after he created plants and animals. It is to ask that man should be reduced to machine programming. It is to ask that man should not exist.

Francis A. Schaeffer, *The God Who Is There,* p. 104.

Friendship

The only way to have a friend
Is to be one yourself.
The only way to keep a friend
Is to give from that wealth.

For friendship must be doublefold;
Each one must give his share
Of feelings true if he would reap
The blessings that are there.

If you would say, "He is my friend,"
Then nothing else will do.
But you must say, "I am his friend,"
And prove that fact be true.

Author Unknown

In the movie, *Only When I Laugh* there are three people who are extremely close friends. One of them says, "The whole world can go to hell if the three of us can have lunch together."

The movie, *Tootsie,* has Michael (portrayed by Dustin Hoffman) masquerading as Dorothy in order to land a dramatic role. In the process he (she) falls in love with Julie and after the masquerade has been exposed wants to continue the relationship on a romantic level as Michael. He says to Julie, "The hard part is over; we're already good friends."

He came up again sputtering and clinging to the wood like a rat, but for all his efforts he could not scramble on top. Every time he tried, the barrel rolled around and ducked him under again. It was really empty and floated light as a cork. Though his ears were full of water, he could hear the elves still singing in the cellar above. Then suddenly the trapdoors fell with a boom and their voices faded away. He was in the dark tunnel, floating in icy water, all alone — for you cannot count friends that are packed up in barrels.

J. R. R. Tolkien, *The Hobbit,* p. 179.

Frustration

Here I sit
With my shoes mismated
Lawdy-mercy!
I's frustrated.
Langston Hughes

Functioning

Unless you can find feeding in the function, you ought not be there.
Richard Niebuhr

Funeral

Nora rejected a wake. She wanted to have a simple funeral the next morning, for only the family. The wonderful boy's body must be quickly and discretely put in the ground without any time for either grief or consolation. Paul agreed, and his tight-lipped brother offered no objections. But Mickey's sisters would not hear of it. Their little brother was to be sent on a long journey to Heaven, and they wanted a spectacular farewell.
Andrew M. Greeley, *Thy Brother's Wife*, p. 214.

Flowers are most often the warmest way people know to express sympathy, and for many they symbolize the flowering of new life even where there is death.
Edgar N. Jackson, *For the Living*, p. 87.

Futility

Herodotus claimed that the bitterest sorrow a man can know is to aspire to do much and achieve nothing. Not so; the bitterest sorrow is to aspire to do much and to do it and then to discover it was not worth doing.
Carlyle Marney

Future

Maslow believes that most individuals have a capacity for

creativeness, spontaneity, caring for others, curiosity, continual growth, the ability to love and be loved, and of the other characteristics found in self-actualized people. A person who is behaving badly is reacting to the deprivation of his basic needs. If his behavior improves he begins to develop his true potential and move toward greater health and normality as a human. Freud, says Maslow, taught us that past experience exists in the present in each individual. "Now we must learn from the growth theory and self-actualization theory that the future also now exists in the person in the form of ideals, hopes, duties, mission, fate, destiny, etc."

Frank Goble, *The Third Force*, p. 53.

"I am a pilgrim of the future," the great Catholic scholar Pierre Teilhard de Chardin used to say. As a paleontologist he had devoted a major part of his life to the study of the past. Although he passionately devoted himself to those studies, an overwhelming vision of God's future permeated all of his works. This is what the Bible does to people; it confronts them with the Word of Promise, recreates them into a people of hope, and sends them on their way into history.

Issac C. Rottenberg, *The Promise and the Presence*, p. 2.

Generosity

Generosity is catching; and if so many men escape it, it is in a great degree from the same reason that countrymen escape the smallpox — because they meet with no one to give it to them.

Lord Greville

Gentleness

I knew it. You are not strict with him, you do not punish him, you do not command him — because you know that gentleness is stronger than severity, that water is stronger than rock, that love is stronger than force.

Herman Hesse, *Siddhartha*, p. 97.

Joe laid his hand upon my shoulder with the touch of a woman. I have often thought of him since like the steam-hammer that can

crush a man or pat an egg-shell, in his combination of strength with gentleness.
Charles Dickens, *Great Expectations,* p. 155.

Giving

A beggar sat on a corner as a large limousine pulled up. very wealthy man in the limousine asked the beggar to share his rice with him. The beggar, very grudgingly gave the rich man three pieces of rice. That night the beggar discovered three pieces of gold in his bowl. He wailed, "If I had only given more."

A person needs three conversions; first of his heart, then of his head, then, lastly, of his purse.
Martin Luther

Do your giving while you're living so you're knowing where it's going.

Legend says that after St. Martin had divided his cloak with a beggar on a wintry November day, summer came back because of his good deed. In France and England, Indian Summer is called St. Martin's Summer.

Then there was the pastor who said right before the offering, "Let your offering be in accordance with your Form 1040."

We have to give ourselves to life
Before we really live.
It's foolish hoarding love or wealth —
They lose, who never give.

There was Psalm 116:12 — "What shall I render to the Lord for all his bounty to me?" That was the question on everyone's mind — "What am I supposed to pledge?" The psalmist seemed to say it was impossible to render anything to the Lord that would match his gifts.
Bob Slosser, *Miracle in Darien,* p. 135.

Goal

In youth I set my goal farther than the eye could see. I am nearer to it now. Or have I moved it nearer to me?
Rebecca McCann

When Margaret Mitchell authored *Gone With the Wind,* she wrote the last chapter first to give her a goal. I understand she wrote her columns for an Atlanta newspaper the same way.

God

I have a little God
And hence my life is small
There is a limit to my dare
My courage and my call
Distinction comes to naught
Between the right and wrong
My visions hover close to earth
While wings disdain my song
My nights are overcast
And through the days I plod
My heart is fain
My hope is gone
I have a little God.
Charles Laymon

The Christian life is not you holding on to God. It is God holding on to you.
Tom Skinner, *Words of Revolution,* p. 129.

This story signifies more than spontaneous combustion or rain-making. Elijah's God was above sharing honors with a sacred cow. God was so conspicious on Mount Carmel that day that Israel started believing all over again.
David A. Redding, *What Is the Man?,* p. 44.

I love the story of the skeptic out walking when he met a farmer. "Where are you going?" asked the skeptic. "I'm going to church to worship God," the farmer replied. With a superior air the skeptic said, "Tell me, sir, is your God a big God or a little God?" "He is both," the farmer answered. "But how can he be both?" the skeptic continued his questions. The farmer answered quickly, "He's so big the heavens cannot contain him and he is so little he lives in my heart." Touché.

There's an Hasidic saying I've believed in for a long time.
"Where does God dwell?"
"Wherever man lets him in."

At Louis XIV's funeral, the cathedral was packed with those who had come to pay respect to their great king. The room was dark except for one candle illuminating the gold casket which held the monarch's remains. The Court Preacher stood to address the people, reached and snuffed out the candle and said, "God only is great."

Sartre speaks of the silence of God.
Heideggar speaks of the absence of God.
Bultmann speaks of the hiddenness of God.
Buber speaks of the eclipse of God.
Tillich speaks of the non-being of God.
Altizer speaks of the death of God.
The New Testament speaks of the love of God.

I find the doing of the will of God leaves me no time for disputing about his plans.
George MacDonald

From the movie, *Chariots of Fire,* I remember this line: "The Kingdom of God is not a democracy; God never seeks re-election."

A man was riding in his car. Suddenly something went wrong and the engine stopped. He checked the engine carefully but could not find anything wrong. As he stood there, another car came into sight. He stopped it and asked for help. A tall man got out, brought some tools and, in short order, had the crippled auto running smoothly. The grateful man asked the stranger's name. It was Henry Ford. The car he had worked on was a Ford. The one who made the Ford knew how to make it run properly. God made you and me. He knows how to make us run properly.

Golden Rule

The Golden Rule is not an adequate guide, not because the ideal is wrong, but because most people do not have enough data about what they want for themselves, or why they want it.
Thomas A. Harris, *I'm O.K. — You're O.K.*, p. 216.

Goodness

In the teaching of Jesus, goodness is not measurable by any yardstick. It is qualitative and not quantitative at all. It is the effort to reproduce the quality of the divine action.
C. H. Dodd, *The Founder of Christianity*, p. 76.

Good News

Christ did not bring the good news. He was the good news.
E. Stanley Jones

Gospel

Thinking of the biblical revelation depicted in the four gospels I recall these words from the musical, *Godspell* when Jesus says, "Pay attention. First read 'em, then heed 'em, you never know when you are going to need 'em."

Gossip

One reason the dog is considered man's best friend is because he wags his tail instead of his tongue.

I've never understood why it's called "idle gossip." It seems to me that gossip is always busy.

Grace

I tried many times to define grace. Here's the best I've been able to come up with: Grace is what you don't deserve but get anyway.

66

Gratitude

Would you know who is the greatest saint in the world? It is not he who prays most or fasts most; it is not he who gives most alms, or is most eminent for temperance, chastity, or justice; but it is he who is always thankful to God, who wills everything that God willeth, who receives everything as an instance of God's goodness, and has a heart always ready to praise God for it.
William Law

God has two dwellings: one in heaven, and the other in a meek and thankful heart.
Isaac Walton

Greed

Two of the worst things that can happen to you are: (1) Not getting what you desperately want and (2) getting it.

Guilt

There is a contrary danger. That is that the orthodox Christian will fail to realize that, at times, guilt-feelings are present when no true guilt exists. Let us remember that the Fall resulted in division not only between God and man, and man and man, but between man and himself. Hence there are psychological guilt-feelings with true guilt. In such cases we must show genuine compassion. But where there is real moral guilt before the God who is there, this must never be passed off or explained away, as the new theology does, as psychological.
Frances A. Schaeffer, *The God Who Is There,* p. 102.

Habit

One good way to break a habit is to drop it.

Handicap

Someone told the story of a beautiful statue in New Mexico which bears the title, "In Spite Of." The name does not honor the subject but the sculptor who suffered an accident and lost his right hand while he was creating the statue. Determined to finish "in spite of" the misfortune, he learned to chisel with his left hand.

Happiness

When choosing your attire for the day, be sure it includes a happy face.

Happiness is the by-product of an effort to make someone else happy.
Gretta Palmer

Rejoice always.
1 Thessalonians 5:16

Hardship

My wife Evelyn and I were having a meeting one night with the graduate students, and I was speaking to them about being down in your spirit, about getting down so low you have to reach up to touch bottom. "I wonder why we get that low?" I asked. "Why do we have to stay in the valley so much?" One young man replied, "Because the soil is better in the valley and that's where the grass grows."
Oral Roberts, *Daily Blessing,* October, 1979, p. 53.

Hate

In Shakespeare's *Romeo and Juliet,* the prince speaks to the two families after the lovers have died, "See what a scourge is laid upon thy hate."

Healing

What we need is a savior and a healer. That is what we have in Jesus Christ. The Greek word, "soter," translated "savior" in the New Testament, means "healer" as well. This is what Jesus is. This is what he was to the paralytic and what he is to us.
Roy C. Clark, *Expect a Miracle,* p. 84.

68

Webster's Dictionary defines "substance" as "That which underlies all outward manifestation; the reality itself; the real essence of a thing." Faith, then, is the real essence out of which healing is done. There is no use in asking God in an uncertain way to do something, because if we ask this we are not giving him the essential material out of which he can do his works. "The prayer of faith shall save the sick." (James 5:15)

Agnes Sanford, *Behold Your God*, p. 29.

I think of Wagner's last opera, when, whenever Parsifal took up the spear used at Christ's Crucifixion and held it against wounds, he had the power to heal.

Hearing

In Genesis we read, "God said." Also in Genesis we read, "the serpent said." Both are still broadcasting. To which are we listening?

Heart

The connection between the heart and the mouth is fascinating to me. When you're frightened, your heart is in your mouth. Often when you fail to speak the appropriate words to another, you experience heartbreak. And you can get awful heartburn when you have to eat your own words.

Heaven

When we are young, heaven is a vague and nebulous place. But as our friends gather there, more and more it gains body and vividness and homeliness. And when your dearest have passed yonder, how real and evident it grows, how near it is.

Arthur John Gossip's Sermon, "When Life Tumbles In, What Then?"

There's the story of a Scottish physician who was attending a close personal friend in his last hours who asked the doctor, "What will it be like after I die?" Just then there was a scratching at the door. The doctor said to his friend, "Hear that? That's my dog. He's been waiting downstairs for me and he's grown impatient. He's never been in this room, has no idea what it's like. He knows only one thing about this room, that I am here. That's all I know about the future — He is there."

Here we listen to five-finger exercises but there we will listen to unimagined symphonies.
George Buttrick, *Christ and History,* p. 39.

Hell

A church member and a visitor were discussing the new minister just after his first sermon —
Visitor: "Why did you ask the other minister to resign?"
Member: "He always preached that if we didn't mend our ways we'd go to hell."
Visitor: "But that's what the new minister preached today."
Member: "I know. But the other one acted as if he were glad of it."

Somewhere C. S. Lewis said, "Hell is a house of mirrors, a reflection of the nature of its occupants."

Helplessness

This recognition and acknowledgment of our helplessness is also the quickest way to that right attitude which God recognizes as essential to prayer. It deals a mortal blow to the most serious sin of all — man's independence that ignores God.
Catherine Marshall, *Adventures in Prayer,* p. 26.

Halleck develops the point that criminality is one of four types of adaptation available for the relief of the sense of helplessness — conformity, activism, and mental illness being the others.
Karl Menniger, *The Crime of Punishment,* p. 178.

Heredity

In studying Jesus' genealogy we learn we are not necessarily victimized or glorified by our ancestors.

"Rehoboam begat Abijam" (a bad father begat a bad son)
"Abijam begat Asa" (a bad father begat a good son)
"Asa begat Jehoshaphat" (a good father begat a good son)
"Jehoshaphat begat Jehoram" (a good father begat a bad son)

Hero

I am nervous about a younger man's high opinion of me. I shared this concern with a confidant who said about the younger man, "He needs a hero." I guess he does but I'm not sure I want it to be me.

History

Everywhere in the past we encounter things which remain unexplained only because they were completely self-understood in their time, and like all daily matters, were not thought necessary to write down.
Jacob Burckhardt

When in Israel I learned that the biggest crime in that country is stealing items from archaelogical ruins. A symbol, I think, of what, in many ways, we do to our history, both intentionally and through neglect.

I am chased headlong back into history by those who profess simply "now" as their alpha and omega.
Malcolm Boyd, *The Lover*, p. 157.

Hockey

A brave hockey player was Chuck.
He had too much bravado to duck.
But, blocking a play
Got his face in the way,
And now he's digesting a puck.

Holiness

How little people know who think holiness is dull. When one

meets the real thing (and perhaps, like you, I have only met it once) it is irresistible. If even 10 percent of the world's population had it, would not the whole world be converted and happy before a year's end?

C. S. Lewis, *Letters to an American Lady,* p. 19.

Holy Spirit

Our problem in the church today is not that we have never heard of the Holy Spirit, but that we have relegated mention of him to Whitsunday or to the repetition of the trinitarian formula.

Lloyd John Ogilvie, *Drumbeat of Love,* p. 237.

When government engineers were engaged in the Tennessee Valley Authority project, the construction of one of the dams was stopped by an old shack that an old mountaineer would not sell for any amount of money. After much insistence from the engineers, the mountaineer told them why he would not move. His grandfather had started a fire in the fireplace which his father, and then he, had never let go out. Knowing this, the engineers ordered a new house be built for the man and one day, when he was out of his shack, they transferred some hot coals from the old fireplace to the one in the new house. They convinced the old man it was the same fire and he moved.

Let us keep Holy Spirit fire burning on the altars of our hearts no matter where we are.

Sean checked his calendar to see what other responsibilities were written in. He was weary and depressed, a weariness that sleep could not cure and a depression that nothing exorcised. He was going through the motions, doing what a priest should do, trying to be what a bishop should be. His self-esteem and self-confidence were shattered, his faith weak, and his hope, at best, paper thin.

Where was the Holy Spirit in his life?

Andrew M. Greeley, *Thy Brother's Wife,* p. 230.

I can't help wondering about the assumption that we can live up to our best ideals without any dynamic from beyond ourselves.

David H. C. Read, *Overheard,* p. 140.

Pentecost is not a spiritual luxury; it is an utter necessity for human living. The human spirit fails unless the Holy Spirit fills.
E. Stanley Jones

Home

Home is the place where, when you have to go there, they have to take you in . . . something you somehow don't have to deserve.
Robert Frost

The home is a place of sacramental relationships where words and ideas are transparent to the depths of God.
David O. Woodyard, *To Be Human Now,* p. 115.

Hope

In August, Mother, Ned, Margot, and I came together for the first time in a year to combine a family reunion with a month's vacation on the shores of Lake Annecy near the Swiss border. The few other guests in the hotel were French, Mother's age or older. On the afternoon of September 1 we all pulled up chairs around the hotel radio to hear Horowitz play Brahm's Second Piano Concerto with the Lucerne Summer Festival Orchestra conducted by Arturo Toscanini. It was good, as someone reminded us, that for a few minutes at least we could forget the threat of war, and someone else pointed to the hope for world peace that must exist when a Russian Jew could play a German concerto with a Swiss orchestra conducted by an Italian-American.
William Sloane Coffin, *Once to Every Man,* p. 22.

There are those who maintain that the situation is too grave for us to do much about it. It was good Moses did not study theology under the teachers of that message; otherwise, I would still be in Egypt building pyramids.
Abraham Joshua Heschel

Thus Israel sought the "land flowing with milk and honey" but found only Palestine where not only milk and honey were flowing but certainly blood and tears. This was not the fulfillment of all hopes, but it was still something. Israel interpreted such experiences of partial fulfillment as an earnest of even greater hopes, as the pledge of an even greater future.

Jürgen Moltmann, *The Experiment Hope,* p. 49.

Life without Jesus is a hopeless end. Life with Jesus is an endless hope.

I stand under an apple tree in blossom and I breathe — this, I believe, this is the single most precious freedom — the freedom to breathe freely as I now can. As long as there is fresh air to breathe under an apple tree after a shower, we may survive a little longer.

Alexander Solzhenitsyn

Human

What I am prepared to do is to claim that Jesus shows us in a way no one ever has what it means to be truly human. Here is the only man who ever got his values straight and who ordered life's priorities as God intended them to be ordered.

Charles Merrill Smith, *How to Talk With God When You're Not Feeling Religious,* p. 141.

Humanism

Beginning from man alone, Renaissance humanism — and humanism ever since — has found no way to arrive at universals or absolutes which give meaning to existence and morals.

Francis A. Schaeffer, *How Should We Then Live?,* p. 55.

Humility

A young preacher looked up from his reading and said to his wife, "How many great preachers do you think there are?" She answered, "I don't know, but there's one less than you think."

When telling thy salvation free,
Let all-absorbing thoughts of thee
My heart and soul engross.
And when all hearts are bowed and stirred

> Beneath the influence of thy word,
> Hide me behind thy cross.
>
> John R. W. Stott, *Between Two Worlds,* p. 335.

Well, I never thought I was God; that's one thing for sure. I grew up wanting to be as good a man as my father was and as my mother wanted me to be. I never had the notion that I was anything special at all; even when I got that job in the White House. And I never had the notion that there weren't a lot of people who couldn't do whatever it was better than I could.

Merle Miller, *Plain Speaking: An Oral Biography of Harry S. Truman,* p. 461.

I even catch this humility in Jesus' resurrection. He does not parade before Pilate, Herod, Caiaphas, and company. He could very well have gone back to the temple to stir the multitudes, or silence the skeptics. No such tactics. His appearances to the disciples could have been announced by heavenly trumpteers and performed with all the impressive splendor of a victorious king. He comes to them quietly at breakfast or dinner time. He joins a couple on a trip. He meets Peter in the lonely, tragic moments after his denial. He is the same Jesus, meek and lowly in heart.

H. S. Vigeveno, *Jesus the Revolutionary,* p. 147.

Humor

Humor not only saves us from ulcers and heart attacks; it, also, saves us from ourselves, from taking ourselves so seriously we can't stand who we are.

Hurry

Hurry means wearing blinders, getting there today without knowing what was missed along the way.

Hypocrisy

In response to the criticism that churches are filled with hypocrites, E. Stanley Jones said, "So what? The hospitals are full of diseased peole and yet are out to banish disease."

E. Stanley Jones, *Conversion,* p. 26.

Did you hear about the two hypocrites who met each other face to face to face to face?

The Pope's new name (John XII) unfortunately did not designate a new character. As Octavian he had in a drunken orgy made a toast to the devil, and as John he continued to live the devil's life. John attended church only when he had a sacerdotal duty to perform and his personal conduct, frequently on public display, was a scandal. However, so far as the records show, his pronouncements on matters of faith were faultless, and his moral teachings were a condemnation of everything for which he stood.
William R. Cannon, *History of Christianity in the Middle Ages*, p. 134.

Ideal

If you can't realize your ideal, idealize your real.

Ideas

All truly wise thoughts have been thought already thousands of times; but to make them truly ours, we must think them over again honestly, till they take root in our personal experience.
Goethe

Identity

In the movie, *Tootsie*, Michael Dorsey masquerading as Dorothy Michaels (both played by Dustin Hoffman) gets hopelessly trapped. Julie thinks "she" is lesbian. Sandy thinks "he" is gay. And Les thinks he is in love with "her."

In the movie, *Reds*, there's this brief dialogue:
"I was wrong about you."
"So was I."

You are haunted by who you are not, who you were meant to be.
Donald Freed, *The Spymaster*, p. 434.

Do you remember the story about the Internal Revenue investigator gathering data in the hill country of Tennessee? He asked a mountain woman, mother of a sizeable family, what was the number of her children. She replied, "They don't have numbers! They all have names!"

Idolatry

In the Holy Bible, atheism is not a threat. Idolatry is. It's the great evil, the big temptation.

Ignorance

I delight in that story which comes out of the ministry of Bishop Francis J. Connell. One of the ministers in a Conference over which the bishop was presiding was visibly perturbed at the church's thoughtlessness in electing a Ph.D., Mr. Connell, to the episcopacy. He concluded his peroration from the floor of the Conference with these words, "Bishop, I am proud of my ignorance." To which the bishop is said to have replied, "Brother, you've got lots to be proud of!"

The obedient proclamation of the intelligent and intelligible Word obliges the church to be particularly on guard against that pious anti-intellectualism with which, in Protestantism at least, we are mightily supplied.

Ernest J. Fieldler and Benjamin J. Garrison, *The Sacraments,* p. 122.

Imagination

The longer I prepare to preach and then do it, the more I'm convinced imagination is a gift of the Holy Spirit.

Impulses

I have learned that, generally speaking, my first impulses are good, right, generous, and, sometimes heroic. That's the Holy Spirit at work in me. However, upon reflection and analysis, I sometimes ignore my first impulses. That's the human spirit (or even the evil spirit) at work in me.

Inadequacy

The late pop singer, Bobby Darin, said he bought elevator shoes because he felt "vertically inadequate." You homileticians ought to have a hey-day with that one.

Inactivity

Most people don't wear out; they rust out.
Colonel Sanders

Incarnation

Somewhere I heard someone say we must follow the spirit of the Incarnation: "We must stoop to conquer."

Christianity has an apt symbol for this unity of God and human, matter and spirit, immanence and transcendence; it's called the Incarnation, literally, "God is flesh."
L. Robert Keck, *The Spirit of Synergy,* p. 105.

When God became a man he demonstrated that he was approachable.
Evan K. Gibson, *C. S. Lewis: Spinner of Tales, p. 143.*

Individualism

The myth of individualism is an ego myth, an Americanism that ain't so. On the other end is the movement craze, the mob that submerges individualism. Ring around the rosey and have community is bogus. What we are about is to renew the Old Testament of community. Have brotherhood without losing individualism and not having to sing the club songs if I don't want to.
Dan Zeluff, *Interpreter's House,* January, 1977.

Inflation

Overheard in a supermarket: "Just get the regular package. We can't afford the economy size."

Influence

Drop a pebble in the water,
And its ripples reach out far;
And the sunbeams dancing on them
May reflect them to a star.

Give a smile to someone passing,
Thereby making his morning glad;
It may greet you in the evening
When your own heart may be sad.

Do a deed of simple kindness;
Though its end you may not see,
It may reach, like widening ripples,
Down a long eternity.
Author Unknown

Instincts

I have found my life to be distinctive when it is instinctive.

Intimacy

I feel my way into intimacy and I hear my way into worth.
Carlyle Marney

Involvement

Billy Sunday had finished an evening service. A man came up to him and said, "Mr. Sunday, I don't like the way you do it." Sunday asked, "How do *you* do it?" The man answered, "Well, I don't." Sunday replied, "Then I like the way I do it better than the way you don't do it."

Jesus

"I do mind, but I suppose I can wait a few days. At least, tell me this — What did Jesus look like?"

"Not as da Vinci, Tintoretto, Raphael, Vermeer, Veronese, or

Rembrandt depicted him, I assure you. Not like the figure of those store-bought religious crosses found in millions of homes throughout the world. James, his brother, knew him as a man, not a martyred matinee idol."

Irving Wallace, *The Word*, p. 106.

When I see what was going on in the life of Jesus going on again in the lives of men, I believe that the experience is worship. And what was going on in the life of Jesus is that persons were becoming more human. In my theology Jesus stands for those events in which men came into their fullest possibilities as human beings, in which they get a hold on their real selves.

David O. Woodyard, *To Be Human Now*, p. 51.

There was a leader once who drove a coach and horses, roughshod, through all the hoary regulations of his culture. He left deep tracks across the smooth surfaces of traditionalism and formalism. He laughed at our legalisms and our lesser sacraments, and his rude steps shattered the sacred pavement of our most precious institutionalism and our prejudiced bigotries. He was a blazing revolutionist, a stout-hearted fighter, and we could take that. But his tools were different: love and a kingdom of love, so we tried to kill him. He overthrew our tables, scattered our coins and livestock, cast out our devils, forgave our prostitutes, and withal, displayed such an unholy disregard for our pigs, law, and culture from Satan. Then he called our best churchmen a "generation of vipers," and our hatred hung out on the line for all to see. He slapped our dead religion and claimed we could not really tell what a fellow is by the way he looks; and worse, he consorted with publicans, sinners, and Samaritans. He insisted that our cultural standards were invalid where they denied human personality its potential, and he rejected the stuff and nonsense of religion so vehemently that it shattered the temple calm. Worst of all, he claimed the primacy of personality so completely that he rejected even the eternity of our temple walls, claimed that God does not have to have us, said he would give us a better temple, and wound up with his glove almost in the face of our high priest! And to all this we had varying reactions.

Carlyle Marney, *Faith in Conflict*, p. 107.

I am an historian and I am a believer. But I must confess, as an historian, this penniless preacher from Galilee is irresistibly the center of history.

H. G. Wells

Great men come and go in history. They make their impact. They achieve eminence and the world acclaims them. Their biographies interpret them. When they are gone their memorials are erected.

Not so with Jesus of Nazareth. Other men appeared and disappeared, but Jesus came upon the stage and has remained there, eternally the same.

Edward L. R. Elson, *And Still He Speaks*, p. 19.

Journey

Somewhere Arnold Toynbee said, "Civilization is a movement and not a condition, a voyage and not a harbor."

Joy

The fruits of the Spirit in Galatians 5:22 are the result of Holy Spirit baptism; they are available to all who are born of the Spirit. And I'm so glad God's given me the second one on the list.

I know a lot of people who talk about being baptized with the Holy Spirit who do not show evidence of the Spirit's fruit, particularly joy. They go through life as if they've been baptized, not in the Spirit, but in pickle juice.

Judgment

God judges us, now and later. I believe he jerks up our behavior for his own precise moral and spiritual scrutiny. I do not believe as H. Richard Niebuhr stated facetiously in a "God without wrath who brings men without sin into a heaven without judgment."

Both times I've visited Paris' Notre Dame I've observed how much its adornment speaks of judgment: those famous devils and gargoyles grinning from its ledges. You can almost see Hugo's hunchback peering and leering from behind every corner.

Someone said that the best fertilizer for any job is the footprints of the boss.
Gene Warr, *You Can Make Disciples,* p. 99.

Justice

The Kingdom of God and social injustice are incompatible.
Gustavo Gutienez

Labels

Society is dying of hardening of the categories. You know about hardening of the arteries — the arteries fill with sludge and grow brittle, impeding blood flow and often causing disability or death. Well, society is dying of hardening of the categories and the church is encouraging the disease.
Phil Barnhart, *Don't Call Me Preacher,* p. 32.

Laity

When we receive new members into our church, I lay hands on them and ordain them to be "ministers of Jesus Christ." I believe in the ministry of the laity.

Laughter

Are you worsted in a fight?
    Laugh it off.
Are you cheated of your right?
    Laugh it off.
Don't make a tragedy of trifles
Don't shoot butterflies with rifles!
    Laugh it off.
Does your work get into kinks?
    Laugh it off.
Are you near all sorts of brinks?
    Laugh it off.

If it's sanity you're after
There's no recipe like laughter.
    Laugh it off.
Author Unknown

Law

The "law" itself can become a substitute for personal encounter with God; it can be the basis for self-righteous defensiveness and avoidance of repentance.
Wayne E. Oates, *Anxiety in Christian Experience*, p. 93.

An unreasoned, unrestricted doing of what comes naturally in any generation leads to personal disorientation and social disorder.
Wallace Fisher, *Stand Fast in Faith*, p. 24.

Lawyers

"You're an unscrupulous, unethical pettifogger!" the prosecutor shouted at the defense lawyer.
"And you're a vicious, poison-tongued liar!"
"Let us proceed with the case," said the judge with a bang of his gavel, "now that the attorneys have been identified."

Life

Sometimes life is a battleground; sometimes a vale of tears; but always it is a vigorous reality.
James T. Cleland

We are born to live, not prepare for life.
Boris Pasternak

For some life is what happens to them while they are making other plans.

Life will either be a mess, a mixture, or a masterpiece.
Kermit L. Long

Life is no brief candle to me. It is a splendid torch which I have got hold of for the moment, and I want to make it burn as brightly as possible before handing it on to future generations.
George Bernard Shaw

I plunge into the day's schedule for, more than once, I have found rapture in the routine.

Limitations

The beginning of growth is when a person accepts his limitations and realizes that he is acceptable in spite of them.
Wayne E. Oates, *Anxiety in Christian Experience,* p. 40.

Listening

Dietrich Bonhoeffer said of our service to others, "The first thing we must do is listen."

Mother Miraim Ruth: "When I was a child I used to speak with my guardian angel . . . anyway, when I was six I stopped listening and my angel stopped speaking."
John Pielmeier, *Agnes of God,* p. 69.

Loneliness

Did you hear about the man who went to the psychiatrist and asked to have his personality split because he was lonely?

It is the pardonable vanity of lonely people everywhere to assume that they have no counterparts.
John LeCarre, *The Honourable Schoolboy,* p. 305.

I took a farewell stroll behind the tracks in that little mountain town, but there was no one to say goodbye to me because no one ever knew that I was there.
Sidney Poitier, *This LIfe,* p. 52.

Lord

An Englishman giving his testimony before a group said, "Up

until now there has been a constitutional monarchy in my spiritual
life. Christ has been King, while I have been the Prime Minister.
But now I have resigned from my position and have made Christ
King, Prime Minister, and Lord of all."
    John T. Seamands, *On Tiptoe With Joy,* p. 39.

Love

How did he define his feeling for Tommaso? Assuredly it was
an adoration of beauty. Tommaso's physical being had a strong
impact on him, gave him a hollow feeling at the pit of his stomach.
He realized that what he felt for Tommaso could only be described
as love; yet he was hardpressed to identify it. Of the loves of his
life, where did this one fit? To which did it compare? It was different from his dependent love for his family, from the reverence
and awe he felt for *Il Magnifico,* his respect for Tertolder; his en-
during though tenuous love for Contessoma; the unforgotten pas-
sion for Clarissa; his friendly love for Granacci; the fatherly love
he felt for Urbino. Perhaps this love, coming so late in his life,
was undefinable.
    Irving Stone, *The Agony and the Ecstasy,* p. 678.

Someone in love class once said, "I wish she could love me
more and need me less."
    Leo Buscaglia, *Love,* p. 71.

Linus said, "I love humanity; it's people I can't stand." But we
have to love in particularity.

God loves each one of us as if there were only one of us.
    Saint Augustine

If love is blind, love cannot hit the mark.
    Shakespeare, *Romeo and Juliet.*

For example, sir, the Bible teaches me that whatever You are,
You are love. I take that to be sound doctrine. So long as I remain convinced that You love me I won't be uptight about my life.
If I know I am loved. I won't be frantic to earn Your love, which
means that I don't have to pretend to a piety I don't possess or lay

claim to a righteousness which a saint couldn't sustain.
Charles Merrill Smith, *How to Talk to God*, p. 211.

On the other hand, the Christian does have the adequate universal he needs in order to be able to discuss the meaning of love. Among the things we know about the Trinity is that the Trinity was before the creation of everything else and that love existed between the persons of the Trinity before the foundation of the world. This being so, the existence of love as we know it in our make-up does not have an origin in chance, but its origin is from that which has always been.
Francis A. Schaeffer, *The God Who Is There*, p. 97.

I've been to Europe twice. The second time I saw about the same things I had the first trip but I experienced so much more. I was with the woman I love.

Man

What can we say about the nature of man from all this? We look around us: We read our history and see a mixed being, neither angel nor demon. He is killer and healer, seeking sometimes the best and sometimes the worst for himself and others. Pope in his "Essay on Man" put it this way:

Born on this Isthmus of a middle state
A being darkly wise and widely great
He hangs between; in doubt to act or rest,
In doubt to deem himself a God or beast,
In doubt his mind or body to prefer,
Born to die and reasoning but to err,
Sole judge of truth in endless error hurled.
The glory, jest, and riddle of the world.

Lawrence LeShan, *How to Meditate*, p. 134.

We cannot have Utopia now;
It's a waste of time to plan it.
For if we had Utopia, how
Would we find the men to man it?
You cannot work the Utopian plan
Unless you have the Utopian man.

Author Unknown

In Paris I saw Rodin's "Adam and Eve" with the figures en-cased in marble straining to emerge from a non-descript mass, providing a parable for our emergence as individuals with specific identity.

Marriage

A husband (or wife) is like a log fire. When left unattended he (she) goes out.

In the play, *Crown Matrimonial*, (dealing with the famous British abdication) Queen Mary says to David, "Stay on the throne and you can change it," to which David replies. "Not without Wallace at my side."

A good wife laughs at her husband's jokes not because they are clever but because she is.

Martin Luther, writing about marriage, said, "He who wants fire will have to put up with some smoke."
Luther's Meditations on the Gospels, p. 43.

As is often the case, the economic anxiety generated in an early marriage became the thing upon which all the other problems of the couple were pegged.
Wayne E. Oates, *Anxiety in Christian Experience*, p. 18.

Henry, please forgive us. I did not know better. I am still so childish that I thought even a married woman had to side with her family. I will never again take sides against you, and I will never again doubt the truthfulness of what you tell me. I love you and I want to live with you the rest of my life."
A sob racked her chest. Henry put his arms around her. "Yes, Sophidion. In the future we must defend ourselves and our mar-riage against all attack."
Irving Stone, *The Greek Treasure*, p. 94.

In a Moslem wedding, a veil is lifted over the bride and groom and sugar is poured through it to symbolize the adding of sweet-ness to the marriage.

A successful marriage is when a couple lives happily *even* after.

Maturity

You are only young once, but you can stay immature indefinitely.

Meaninglessness

Sometimes abstraction was saying that there was nothing to say. Gallery visitors scratching their heads and asking each other, "But what does it mean?" were interpreting the painting exactly as the painter had in mind for them to do. He was asking of life that very same question and he was getting the very same no answer. In confronting the meaningless painting, one came to understand a meaningless world.

Mary Jean Irion, *From the Ashes of Christianity*, p. 105.

Mediocrity

Only a mediocre person is always at his best.

Meditation

The road of meditation is not an easy one. The first shock of surprise comes when we realize how undisciplined our mind really is; how it refuses to do the bidding of our will. We realize that if our bodies were half as unresponsive to our will as our minds are, we would never get across the street alive.

Lawrence LeShan, *How to Meditate*, p. 14.

We have been so busy in Christianity in recent years that we've stopped meditating. Now the fashionable Eastern religions are teaching the younger generation to be still and know that God is God and to meditate.

Martin Marty

The method developed by St. Sulpice can be very helpful in biblical meditation. The three movements in this approach to meditation are:

Christ before my eyes — adoration
Christ in my heart — communion
Christ in my hands — cooperation
Ben Johnson, *Experiencing Faith,* p. 36.

Memory

The old house seems bigger to me now in memory than it must have been.
Rod McKuen, *Finding My Father,* p. 25.

Mercy

I often visited, pastorally, at Saint Joseph's Hospital in Atlanta. The elevator doors have the word mercy embossed in large brass letters. Every time the elevator opened I thought of how wide open God's mercy has been in my life.

Middle-Age

That difficult period between adolescence and retirement when you have to take care of yourself.

Ministry

You are my people, given me to love,
To serve, to shepherd thru the days ahead;
I pray God that I may be worthy of
This honor; I am glad that I was led
To come to you, that thru God's gentle grace
My lines have fallen in this gentle place.

I would be strong to work where there is need;
I would be true to serve you as I should;
And I would give the Bread of Life to feed
Each hungry soul who comes to me for food;
And I would honor with my every word
The blessed Savior — Jesus Christ our Lord.

I plead with you for patience. Should I make
An error, I would gladly make amends,

Or if some unintentional mistake
Be mine, I crave your understanding, friends.
As pastor and as people may we be
Builders together for Eternity.
Grace Noll Crowell

Brothers in Christ, we have been called by God to be faithful priests and not successful salesmen. The "St." before the names of the apostles stands for "Saint" not "statistician." Indeed it is only because they were saints and not statisticians that they were able to look upon a 5 ft. 10 in., 165 lb. hooknosed Jew hanging on a cross — and call it a divine victory rather than a human defeat. I sometimes wonder what Jesus' annual congregational report would have looked like if he had made one out on Good Friday afternoon. Certainly there would be little there to justify his promotion to a growing suburb of Jerusalem, to say nothing of Pittsburgh or New Delhi.
William H. Lazareth

He actually managed to make new sallies out of the Vatican into the center of Rome, as in the old days. It was as though he didn't want to lose his nickname by which the Romans knew him: "John-outside-the-walls."
S. C. Lorit, *Everybody's Pope,* p. 220.

My dear friend, Maynard Jackson, former mayor of Atlanta and the son of a Baptist pastor said to me, "Politics is my ministry."

Miracles

Though the story of Dives and Lazarus has been described as the harshest of Jesus' parables, it is, in fact, one of the most hopeful. For I am Lazarus and so are you, and we have Jesus' word for it that our vulnerability and dependence place us squarely within the zone of miracles.
Colin Morris, *The Hammer of the Lord,* p. 43.

We lift Christ's teaching out of miracles but New Testament people looked on miracles as supporting the teachings. What he said had to have what he did to go with it.
William R. Cannon

Missions

The Christian dare not give rice freely for the belly and withhold the pure milk of the Gospel for the soul.
Donald McGavaran, *Understanding Church Growth*, p. 150.

Mistakes

I saw a man recently who has not made a mistake in 4,000 years. He's a mummy in the Cairo, Egypt museum.

Morality

The best prevention for moral decay is brushing up on the absolute laws of Almighty God.

In our confused society — which cannot or will not distinguish between right and wrong — no-fault morality is gaining ground.
Wallace Fisher, *Stand Fast in Faith*, p. 64.

Mothers

In the movie, *Kiss Me Good-Bye*, the interior decorator says to Kay (portrayed by Sally Fields), "Your mother's driving me mad."
Kay replies, "Pretend she's your mother and ignore her."

The thing that automatically does all the work while you just sit there is now called automation. It used to be called Mother.

Motivation

Motivation is a big word these days. A mother was trying to get her little boy to eat his cereal and he said, "Motivate me, Mom."

Music

A man just back from the city was telling his wife of the church he had attended. "Did you know any of their songs?" she asked.

"No," replied the man. "They didn't sing anything but anthems."
"Anthems!" exclaimed his wife, "What on earth is an anthem?"
"Well," answered the man, "I can't tell you just exactly, but if I'd say to you, 'Betsy, the cows are in the corn,' that would not be an anthem. But if I'd say, 'Betsy, Betsy, Betsy, the cows, the cows, the Holstein cows, the mully cow, the Jersey cow, the spotted cow — all the cows are in, are in, the corn, corn, corn ah-men.' why, that'd be an anthem."

Johann Sebastian Bach (1685-1750) was certainly the zenith of the composers coming out of the Reformation. His music was a direct result of the Reformation culture and the biblical Christianity of the time, which was so much a part of Bach himself. There would have been no Bach had there been no Luther. Bach wrote on his score initials representing such phrases as: "With the help of Jesus" — "To God alone be the glory" — "In the name of Jesus." It was appropriate that the last thing Bach the Christian wrote was "Before Thy Throne I Now Appear." Bach consciously related both the form and the words of his music to biblical truth.
Francis A. Schaeffer, *How Should We Then Live?* p. 92.

Mystery

I went to the B'nai temple in Havla, Israel and learned their religion is based on the theory that all religions believe in the same God but have no understanding. You can be a Christian, a Jew, etc. but B'nai has total understanding. I left the temple talking to myself saying, "But we're not supposed to understand all; there's always mystery surrounding God. His face is always concealed from us, to some degree."

Thank God for the mystery! Mystery implies sovereignty, demands faith, and anticipates relevation!

Mysticism

"I don't know what you think of me," she said, speaking slowly. "Many people associate me with a spiritualism. But that's wrong. Yes, I think I have a gift," she continued quietly. "But it isn't occult. In fact, to me it seems natural, perfectly natural. Being a

Catholic, I believe that we all have a foot in two worlds. The one that we're conscious of is time. But now and then a freak like me gets a flash from the other foot; and that one, I think . . . is in eternity."

William Peter Blatty, *The Exorcist*, p. 88.

Nature

I love to watch
God paint the dawn
In scarlet flush and gold;
I love to watch
Him touch the sky
In colors bright and bold.
I love to watch
God paint the dusk
In purple-shadowed gray.
Then leave his name
Upon it all . . .
Artist of night and day.

Marion Schoeberlein

Need

Hark, hark, the dogs do bark
The beggars are coming to town
Some in rags
Some in tags
And some in velvet gowns.

Nursery Rhyme

In the play, *Two for the Seesaw*, Jerry Ryan needs to be needed. He says to Gittel Mossa, "Make a claim, a real claim — you may be surprised."

Jesus wants us to come to him with our needs. John 7:37 says, "If any man thirst, let him come to me and drink." He provides the living water but we provide the thirst.

But let's not get our needs and wants mixed up.

Nervous

In the movie, *Starting Over,* the hero (portrayed by Burt Reynolds) has an anxiety attack in a department store. His brother hurries to the scene to help and asks the crowd, "Does anyone have a valium?" The whole crowd opens up purses and pockets and throws dozens of pills at him. This scene serves as cryptic commentary about a society missing the inner peace of life controlled by the presence of the Holy Spirit.

New

In 1967 Dr. Christian Barnard made medical history by performing the first successful heart transplant. After the patient recovered, he asked Dr. Barnard to let him see his old heart. Dr. Barnard brought it to him in a jar and let him hold it. After looking at his old heart for a couple of minutes, the patient said, "Doctor, thank you for taking away my old diseased heart and giving me a new one."

The idea of heart transplant is not new, is it? "And I will give you a new heart. I will take out your stony hearts of sin and give you new hearts of love." (Ezekiel 36:26)

New Birth

Jesus himself was born without human generation, being conceived by the Holy Spirit; and something like that has to happen to those who would enter the family of God. We must be born again by the action of God.

Everett L. Fullum, *Living the Lord's Prayer,* p. 32.

In Genesis we read, "God breathed into man and he became a living soul." Taken at face value, that says the breath of God is life. To stop breathing is to die — to be separated from the life of the body. Life depends on the process of breathing. New life in a person — resurrection life — is having God breathe again into us. What happens then in this "new birth" experience is like getting a second life.

James Kilgore, *Being Up in a Down World,* p. 82.

Obedience

In his book, *Agenda for Biblical People,* Jim Wallis points out that "the great tragedy of modern evangelism is in calling many to belief but few to obedience."

Jesus said His yoke is easy. True, but only if, when yoked to Him, I am going in the same direction He is.

Old

I don't know what it's like
To be old —
But I think —
It's living long enough
To make a joke of the things
That were once
Breaking your heart —

Merritt Malloy, *Things I Meant to Say to You When We Were Old,* p. 57.

Opportunity

I love the words from the song, "Moon River":
"Two drifters off to see the world;
there's such a lot of world to see."
There is, isn't there, much of it right at your doorstep.

Many do with opportunities as children do at the seashore; they fill their little hands with sand, and then let the grains fall through, one by one, till all are gone.

Thomas R. James

Optimism

It's really a wonder that I haven't dropped all my ideals, they seem so absurd and impossible to carry out. Yet I keep them because in spite of everything I still believe that most people are really good at heart.

Anne Frank

Pain

And a woman spoke, saying, "Tell us of Pain." And he said: "Your pain is the breaking of the shell that encloses your understanding. Even as the stone of the fruit must break, that its heart may stand in the sun, so must you know pain. And could you keep your heart in wonder at the daily miracles of your life, your pain would not seem less wondrous than your joy."

Kahlil Gibran, *The Prophet,* p. 58.

Parents

"Would to God that your mother could be with you." The heat of his words caused her to lift her head. They regarded each other, facing the truth. "Or some woman. I can't leave you, Mary. And if the midwife doesn't come — I'm but a man, without knowledge of these things."

"Don't be afraid," she gripped his hand. "We're forgetting something. That this is God's child and God will not abandon us. Weak and human as we are God has chosen us to be his servants. Surely he will help us."

Marjorie Holmes, *Two From Galilee,* p. 197.

In a Eugenia Price book, Horace is going home, not at all sure of his reception. He speaks: "If there really was a God, he who decided human relationships; he had certainly worked out a strange arrangement with parents and their offspring."

Eugenia Price, *New Moon Rising,* p. 4.

Past

Sometimes we are chained to the past like the circus elephant that always stood in one spot. Was he tied up? No. He just thought he was.

> The goofus bird flew backward
> Over river, moor, and fen.
> He doesn't care where he is going
> But wants to know
> Where he has been.

Ruby Flowers

It never pays to waste time looking back at the doors of life which have closed behind one. New doors are always opening ahead. They are the important ones.

Anonymous

The past calls for two basic attitudes and actions: repentance for the evil and gratitude for the good.

Nels F. S. Ferre, *The Extreme Center,* p. 21.

Pastor

At our church retreat I was sharing my need to be spiritually fed and our retreat director, Ben Johnson, replied, "Unless the shepherd gets fed, he'll eat the sheep."

There's the story of a few people in a congregation trying to get support to dismiss the pastor because of his stand on certain social issues. They went to the most influential man in the congregation, whom they knew opposed the pastor's stand and asked him to vote against the pastor. He refused and they were confused. "Why won't you vote against him?" "Because," he replied, "When my wife was dying he held her hand for the last twenty-four hours and held mine for the next twenty-four hours."

Patience

Geology gives us an understanding of the patience of God.

Josiah Gilbert Holland

Peace

With eager heart and will on fire,
I fought to win my great desire.
"Peace shall be mine," I said; but life
Grew bitter in the weary strife.

My soul was tired, and my pride
Was wounded deep; to Heaven I cried,
"God grant me peace or I must die."
The dumb stars glittered no reply.

Broken at last, I bowed my head,
Forgetting all myself, and said,
"Whatever comes, His will be done,"
And in that moment peace was won.
Henry Van Dyke

Following a long study of wars inside and outside myself, I have learned that the fundamental prerequisite of any contribution I can make to world peace is the establishment of equilibrium at the center of my own life.
Malcolm Boyd, *The Lover,* p. 158.

Perseverance

Fight one more round. When your feet are so tired that you have to shuffle back to the center of the ring, fight one more round. When your arms are so tired that you can hardly lift your hands to come on guard, fight one more round. When your nose is bleeding and your eyes are black and you are so tired that you wish your opponent would crack you one on the jaw and put you to sleep, fight one more round — remembering that the man who always fights one more round is never whipped.
James J. Corbett

Pessimism

Don't put in so much time preparing for a rainy day that you have no time to enjoy the sunny ones.

Pharisees

Herzog could see that Edvig was fascinated by every word about Madeline. Nodding, he raised his head, his chin rose at every sentence, he touched his neat beard, his lenses glittered, he smiled. "You feel she's a Christian?"

"She feels I'm a Pharisee. She says so."

"Ah?" Edvig sharply commented.

"Ah, what?" Moses said. "You agree with her?"

"How can I? I scarcely know you. But what do you think of the question?"

"Do you think that any Christian in the twentieth century has the right to speak of Jewish Pharisees? From a Jewish standpoint, you know, this hasn't been one of your best periods."
Saul Bellow, *Herzog.* p. 71.

Planning

Noah leaned on the gunwale of the Ark, gazing glumly down into the deep green sea. "I could kick myself," he said.

"What's the matter?" replied Mrs. Noah.

"Poor planning," he said, waving his hand toward the waters. "More fish out there than any other living thing — and we only brought two worms!"

Pleasure

More than once he describes God as a hedonist at heart. This derogatory word, which usually means one who spends his life seeking and enjoying pleasure, is used ironically to express a great truth about the divine nature. The love which is at the heart of the Trinity, of course, produces pleasure — pleasure for all creatures who are in harmony with God.
Evan K. Gibson, *C. S. Lewis: Spinner of Tales,* p. 108.

Politics

A politician, a surgeon, and an engineer were arguing over whose profession was first established.

"Mine was," said the surgeon. "The Bible says that Eve was created by excising a rib from Adam."

"But before that," said the engineer, "a six-day engineering job created the earth out of chaos."

"Aha," said the politician. "But who created the chaos?"

Pollution

It's a dirty shame that there's so much pollution.

Someone said that the beautiful pink flamingoes of Florida stand around on one leg because they can't stand the thought of putting both feet in the water.

Potential

"But I am potentially a sinner at all times," a clergyman once said to me, apparently forgetting that on the previous Sunday he had asked the life of Christ to come into him and take away his sin.

"You are, also, potentially a saint at all times," I reminded him, "but it is hard for his Holy Spirit to make you a saint if you fasten your attention upon being a sinner."

Agnes Sanford, *Behold Your God*, p. 52.

Praise

If I just had a piano,
if I just had an organ,
if I just had a drum,
how I could praise my Lord!

But I don't need no piano,
    neither organ
        nor drum
for to praise my Lord!
Langston Hughes

Prayer

The man who starts his day on bended knee is less likely to end it on bended elbow.

We need to mobilize a new army of ten million and train them to use a weapon as powerful for peace as rocket bombs were for destruction. Other weapons converted enemies into skeletons. This weapon must convert enemies into friends. It must heal the horrid open wound which bombs have left across the face of the world. Only prayer, which releases the infinite might of God, can win this final battle for men's hearts and minds.

Frank Laubach, *Prayer*, p. 14.

In-depth prayer for people liberates us to enjoy them right now, where they are, as they are. William Law was right: "There's nothing which makes us love a man so much as praying for him."

And prayer-born love frees us to recognize that the person is himself God's greatest answer to prayer.

Lloyd John Ogilvie, *Drumbeat of Love*, p. 158.

If we are so busy with important things that we do not have time to pray an hour a day, then we are so busy that we need to pray two hours a day.

St. Francis de Sales

One of my students made an interesting remark after re-reading the Book of Acts. "We're so busy," he said, "that we have to interrupt what we're doing in order to pray. But God was always having to interrupt the first Christians at their prayer in order to get them to do things."

John Killinger, *Bread for the Wilderness, Wine for the Journey*, p. 48-49.

I have a friend who, after twelve years, has been released from prison. In one of the many letters he wrote me he, speaking of his church praying for him, said: "I have felt all along the cord unwinding from the spool."

God answers sharp and sudden on some prayers and thrusts the thing we have prayed for in our face.

Elizabeth Barrett Browning

Prayer, mind you, is not an effort to affect the will of God but to discover it.

Sam Shoemaker

I will think more of your prayers when I see more of your praises.

Robert Louis Stevenson

Preaching

Shoot us, shake us, then soothe us.
Jess Moody, *A Drink at Joel's Place*, p. 99.

An Indian had this to say about a sermon: "High wind, big thunder, no rain."

Preaching needs to be earthly but not crass.
Bishop Bryan

It was Donne's last pastorate and would last ten years. He was to die, almost literally in the pulpit.

His preaching surpassed his promise. Great crowds came and men made their confession. Even his leery old cronies detected no taint of deceit. Donne preached "to," not "at." Here was no stranger to sin, but a man who had known lust, ambition, pride, hate firsthand. He did not set himself up as a saint on a pedestal but as a prodigal returned. When he prayed, he prayed that he might be forgiven "that by thy mercy to my sin, other sinners may see how much sin thou canst pardon."
David A. Redding, *What Is the Man?* p. 132.

The preacher's little daughter had been standing by his desk, watching him write Sunday's sermon. "Father," she asked after a while, "didn't you tell me once that God tells you what to put in your sermon?"

"Yes, dear."

"Then why do you scratch so much of it out?"

Seldom if ever can the pew rise higher than the pulpit.
John R. W. Stott, *Between Two Worlds*, p. 115.

Predecessor

The real challenge, of course, was to succeed Sidney Lovett. For twenty-six years he had been pastor to a whole community — students, faculty, other Yale employees and their families, to citizens of New Haven of every stripe of belief. I knew I could take only his job; no one could take his place.
William Sloane Coffin, *Once to Every Man*, p. 133.

Prejudice

"If I ever need a heart or brain transplant," said a comedian, "I want the donor to be a bigot. That way I'll get a heart or brain that's never been used."

Presence

Recently Skip spoke at a meeting and I found his words helpful. Our Sunday School class sat around a campfire after a weiner roast. Skip shared with us his own struggles as a Christian. "I've learned that it's a two-way street," he said. "I used to think that walking with the Lord meant that I had to run up the hill in order to meet God who was up there waiting for me. Recently, I've decided that while I am running up, God is coming to meet me."

Cecil Murphey, *Seven Daily Sins,* p. 93.

Present

When I came into the business, one of the people I admired was the writer Walter "Red" Smith. I got to know him and he gave two words of advice on how to do my job. "Be there!"

Howard Cosell, *Cosell,* p. 136.

Price

The price of bacon these days gives you an idea of what's meant by the term, hog wild.

Pride

A man with insomnia went to a psychiatrist. He was staying awake solving the world's problems. On a subsequent visit, he said, "I'm not staying awake any more solving the world's problems. Now I'm staying awake because of the ticker-tape parades given in my honor because I have solved them."

Priest

What is the function of a priest? Briefly, the chief responsibility of a priest is to bring God to man and man to God in a life-giving relationship.

Charles M. Laymon, *They Dared to Speak for God,* p. 30.

Priority

In the musical, *Applause,* Margo sees her age obsession for what it is. She sees her profession for what it is. She sees Bill and sings, "There's Something Greater."

Thus all that fall and winter — one of the most frigid years within living memory — I found how swiftly the body loses its sap and the soul its optimism through having one's energies split three dozen ways.
William Stryon, *The Confessions of Nat Turner,* p. 241.

Problems

It is given to many men to see the problems of our day — it is given to very few to have the courage to do something about them.
Albert Einstein

Procrastination

I love the T-shirt somebody gave me. It says "Tomorrow I am going to quit procrastinating."

Progress

When Bishop Ainsworth retired from the Methodist episcopacy he said this to Bishop Cannon who was entering the episcopacy: "Son, my face is toward the horizon where the sun never sets."

Someone asked David Livingstone where he was prepared to go and he said: "Anywhere, as long as it is forward."

Promises

With the call of God comes the promise to provide all that is necessary to carry out that call.
Bob Slosser, *Miracle in Darien,* p. 153.

I have encountered many challenges in my life that are fraught with peril but full of promise.

Prophet

I read a book on Billy Graham where his fifth grade teacher had been interviewed. She said when Billy was in her class he was so shy she couldn't get him to respond. Years later when she saw him preaching on television, she said: "I kept thinking that somebody had to be putting the words in his mouth."

Protest

The highest form of protest is to build the new, not to fight the old.

David Spangler, *Revelation: The Birth of a New Age*, p. 167.

Providence

Often people, knowing I'm a minister, ask me if I can do anything about foul weather. I reply: "I'm in sales, not management."

On an Arabic plane to Jordan, I asked a Saudi what the inscription on the airplane wall meant. He translated it for me: "This plane operates because of God."

Punishment

Betsy's grandmother told her they didn't have television when she was a little girl. The four-year-old was quiet for a moment, then said, "What did they turn off when you were bad?"

Purity

Purity of heart is to will one thing. It is to eliminate all other masters.

Soren Kierkegaard

Purpose

And from somewhere, I heard a victorious "Yes" in answer to my question of the existence of an ultimate purpose.

Victor Frankl, *Man's Search for Meaning*, p. 63.

We have the sense that we are getting nowhere far too fast and that, if something doesn't happen soon, we may arrive.
Archibald MacLeish

As long as what we are fighting for, or fighting against has meaning, we can get the hell kicked out of us and still not lose the light in our eyes.
James W. Angell

Questions

Fortune-teller: "I charge 10 dollars for two questions."
Customer: "Isn't that high?"
Fortune-teller: "Yes. Now what's your second question?"

An answer is only an answer for one who is asking a question.
Roy C. Clark, *Expect a Miracle,* p. 87.

Race Relations

One of my favorite people in Atlanta, Georgia, is Dr. Williams Holmes Borders, pastor of the Wheat Street Baptist Church. I'll never forget the evening Dr. Borders, a black man, preached in the church I pastored and said: "Either we go up together or we go down together." Simple but profound, don't you think?

Which reminds me of the time I heard Martin Luther King, Jr.'s daughter say: "We may not have all come over in the same ship but, now, we are all in the same boat."

Realism

The dwarves forgot their joy and their confident boasts of a moment before and cowered down in fright. Smavg was still to be reckoned with. It does not do to leave a live dragon out of your calculations, if you live near him.
J. R. R. Tolkien, *The Hobbitt,* p. 207.

And I came across as a human being, not some sort of a facsimile person, the way some performers do in shows that are

filmed and refilmed, and edited and cut and fixed up until they have about as much humanity as a plastic puppet.
Liberace, *Liberace: An Autobiography*, p. 98.

I don't know where I heard it but I surely like it: "Jesus saw life with the lid off."

In the movie, *Ordinary People*, the son says to his father, "Everything's jello pudding with you, Dad. You don't see things."

Reason

Always there is the tug of war between wonder and reason, until the heart decides the victor.
Margaret Abbott

Receiving

I've had a difficult time receiving. My friend Ben Johnson helped me when he said: "There can be no blessed givers if there are no blessed receivers."

God blesses us. Let's stop talking and start taking.

Redemption

Man and sin are the necessary antecedents of Christ and redemption.
William R. Cannon, *Evangelism in a Contemporary Context*, p. 41.

The great Christian word is redemption, which means transforming a destructive relationship into one in which the conditions and purposes of love are realized. Let us remember that fine linen paper is made out of old dirty rags.
Reuel L. Howe, *Herein Is Love*, p. 58.

Relationship

Watching the television program, *Love Boat*, one evening, this line struck me: "I'm much better at romance than I am at relationship."

> Living depends on loving,
> loving depends on knowing,
> knowing depends on risking.

Maxie Dunnam, *Dancing at My Funeral*, p. 18.

Sometimes our light goes out but is blown into flame by an encounter with another human being. Each of us owes the deepest thanks to those who have rekindled this inner light.

Albert Schweitzer

Relativity

Relativity is why the red light is twice as long as the green light even though both are twenty seconds.

Religion

Someone said that when St. Paul got converted, he lost his religion. What do you think?

A bizarre scene occurred on a street corner in Ann Arbor, Michigan, as two men stood, arguing with each other. One wore a sandwich board proclaiming himself a disciple of a currently popular "guru." The other had a bucket full of publications of a rival cult. And the crowds passed by, casting bemused glances in their direction.

Repentance

What response to the challenge did Jesus expect from his hearers? "The Kingdom of God is upon you; repent!" The word "repent" in English suggests being "sorry for your sins." That's not what the Greek word means. It means, quite simply, to think again, to have second thoughts, to change your mind. "Repentance," as the gospels mean it, is a readjustment of ideas and emotions, from which a new pattern of life and behavior will grow (as the "fruit of repentance").

C. H. Dodd, *The Founder of Christianity*, p. 58.

Resolutions

Be it resolved that I will:

Like Paul, forget those things which are behind and press forward.

Like David, lift my eyes to the hills from whence my help comes.

Like Abraham, trust my God implicitly.

Like Moses, suffer rather than enjoy the pleasure of sin for a time.

Like Job, be patient and faithful in all circumstances.

Like Joseph, turn my back on all evil advances.

Like Gideon, advance even when my friends are few.

Like Andrew, strive to lead my brother to Christ.

Response

I heard of a pastor who visited a parishioner who had just been crippled by a serious accident.

The pastor expressed sympathy, "An accident like that really colors life."

"Yes," replied the parishioner, "But I intend to choose the color."

Resurrection

Tomb, thou shalt not hold Him longer;
Death is strong, but Life is stronger;
Stronger than the dark, the light,
Stronger than the wrong, the right:
Faith and Hope triumphant say,
Christ will rise on Easter Day.
Phillips Brooks

Without Resurrection, the Cross is Devil's work, and Christ a tragic victim. What else but the Resurrection could have written the New Testament? That Book, which even our largely pagan culture cannot escape, is not a dirge sung around a grave, but a shout of joy around a conquered grave.
George Buttrick, *Christ and History,* p. 132.

At Gordon's Tomb in Jerusalem I saw a plaque that said, "Enter with reverence. Leave with a smile. He's not here."

C. S. Lewis was asked what he would do if he knew that a nuclear bomb had been launched. He replied that in the fraction of a second before the dropping of the bomb and its detonation, a man would still have time to say to himself, "Pooh! You're only a bomb. I'm an immortal soul!"

Revelation

Of all the contents revealed by God the most important by far is God himself.

L. Harold DeWolf

But the old man only smiled patiently. "Doris, my dear, I have told you before and I'll tell you again. The Lord reveals himself in many ways. So long as good men are prepared to go out and seek for truth and justice and brotherly love, He'll not be kept waiting too long outside the door."

John LeCarre, *The Honourable Schoolboy*, p. 247.

Revival

Although Aldersgate (in my opinion) was inevitable, it also was absolutely necessary for Wesley both as a Christian and an evangelist. Aldersgate did not so much make him great, for the ingredients for greatness were already there; it made him useful. Adlersgate made Wesley a Christian in the full sense of the word and directed his greatness to the needs of the people. Aldersgate was necessary for revival. Without it, Wesley would not have known an effect upon man beyond his own special gifts. Revival is the work of God through men, not of men alone. No matter how great, Wesley would not trust God for the change he had so diligently sought to create himself. Again, Aldersgate was not only necessary for him personally, but for his ministry among others as well.

Robert G. Tuttle, Jr., *John Wesley, His Life and Theology*, p. 217.

Revival is nothing else than a new obedience to God.
Charles G. Finney

Revolution

Far too often Christians have allowed the faith to appear as a reactionary influence in a revolutionary world, whereas the truth is the exact reverse. It is secularism that is reactionary; Christianity, when authentic, is revolutionary enough, as the Book of Acts reminds us, to "turn the world upside down." And indeed, all through the centuries, in the name of Christ men have marched right up to some of the most formidable, virulent social evils, crying, "It is not the will of God that we should tolerate this hateful tyranny one moment longer: It is the will of God that we should destroy it!" — and there and then the axe has been laid to the root of the noxious tree, and the hideous abuse has been crashed to its destruction.

James S. Stewart, *The Wind of the Spirit,* pp. 50-51.

Right

In the play, *Bus Stop,* Dr. Gerald Lyman, drunken former professor says: "Sometimes it's so gratifying to do the right thing that I wonder I don't choose to do it always."

Sacrament

The two sacraments of Baptism and the Lord's Supper are divinely appointed visual aids, "visible words," dramatizing the grace of God in salvation through Christ.

John R. W. Stott, *Between Two Worlds,* p. 78.

Sacred

Nothing here below is profane for those who know how to see; on the contrary, everything is sacred.

Pierre Tielhard de Chardin

Salvation

I think we need to use the name Jesus more. Not just Christ

or Lord but Jesus — "He who saves." Saving is what we need and Jesus is our Savior.

He did not come first of all to give us knowledge or to show his wisdom and power. He came to set us free from sin; to heal us; to save us; to overcome our alienation from himself; to establish fellowship with us and among men within the presence and the power of love.

Nels F. S. Ferre, *Know Your Faith*, p. 46.

Anything's possible. What does the governor know about people like these? No man is ruined forever. No matter what he's done, there comes a moment in his life when he can be saved, when he can be made into someone good and useful to the community.

Henri Charriere, *Papillion*, p. 441.

Sanctification

Justification leads inevitably to sanctification. Doctrine without duty is sterile; faith without works is dead.

John R. W. Stott, *Between Two Worlds*, p. 155.

Science

Science observes and proves the survival of the fittest but cannot account for the arrival of the fittest.

Carlyle Marney, *Faith in Conflict*, p. 25.

Second Coming

Will He come in the twilight
When the day is done
And send as His herald
The setting sun?

Will He come at dawning
When the world awakes
And all the sweetness
Of the morning takes?

Will it be at noontime
When life runs high

With the sun's bright banner
In the midday sky?

Morning, noon, or evening
When, we do not know;
Let us then be ready
When He comes, to go.
Author Unknown

Seeking

Some questions are put to us not so we can answer them but so we can struggle with them.

I'll never forget what my friend Doug Chase said when we were asked why we had come on a retreat sponsored by our church: "I have come here to seek the Lord's face."

Self

The great Jewish scholar, Bousha, said that when he met God in heaven He would not say, "Bousha, why were you not like Moses?" God would say, "Bousha, why were you not like Bousha?"

I'm saying, I suppose, that there is a part of me I haven't been in touch with yet, and from all indications I have every reason to fear an introduction.
Sidney Poitier, *This Life*, p. 77.

There is a way in which running yourself down is irreverent. It says God didn't give you what it takes.

You are the best you. You'll always be the second best anyone else.
Leo Buscaglia, *Love*, p. 23.

Self-Centered

The man who lives by himself and for himself is apt to be corrupted by the company he keeps.
Charles Henry Parkhurst

Haven't you learned yet never to argue with Sammy about himself?" she said. "That's one subject on which I'm convinced he is infallible."

Budd Schulberg, *What Makes Sammy Run?*, p. 67.

Service

It's one thing to want the Holy Spirit so you can use Him; it's another thing to want Him so He can use you.

John T. Seamands, *On Tiptoe With Joy!*, p. 89.

Oh, we are willing to follow His footsteps to the Mount of Transfiguration, to some other great height, to some glimpse of glory! But when they lead through the dark dungeons of service, such as foot-washing, then we hang back and are not willing to follow His example. If we do not serve, however, we are none of His.

Earl K. Allen, *Trials, Tragedies and Triumphs*, p. 38.

Life can never be dull again
When once we've thrown the windows open wide
And seen the mighty world that lies outside,
And whispered to ourselves this wondrous thing,
"We're wanted for the business of the King!"

Author Unknown

Sharing

Joy shared is a double delight, and sorrow shared is only half a burden.

My brother and I (the Berrigan brothers) have wanted, as Phil puts it, to "share our lives." And it is interesting, I think, and very profound on his part, that he calls that the revolution — sharing one's life with others.

Robert Coles, *The Geography of Faith*, p. 149.

Silence

The bench wasn't any too comfortable, but he didn't seem to

notice; he pulled out a pipe and lighted it without any of the affectations; his thoughts felt far away and once or twice he ran his hand through his hair so that it stood up like a stubble of wheat, and I was falling under the spell of his silence. A man who can keep a thought-filled and active silence for more than two minutes can hold anyone for two hours.

Adela Rogers St. Johns, *Tell No Man*, p. 66.

Sin

In fact, the anxiety of sin is a special type of grief situation in that the individual is separated and estranged from his meaningful community by his sin. He has lost communication with those who mean most to him, and this is true even in terms of his relationship to God.

Wayne E. Oates, *Anxiety in Christian Experience*. p. 68.

In the movie, *Best Little Whorehouse in Texas*, Mona says to Ed Earl, "Some people confuse sin and the law."

But most of us are probably like William Temple, the late Archbishop of Canterbury. As a student at Oxford, he went to hear a famous American evangelist. The preacher pressed upon his student congregation the forgiveness of God, quoting the text, "Though your sins be as scarlet, they shall be as white as snow." Temple said, "Though I went to the meeting in a serious, inquiring spirit, I found myself quite unmoved, for, alas, my sins were not scarlet, they were gray, all gray. They were not dramatic acts of rebellion — but the colorless, tired sins of omission, inertia, and timidity."

Robert T. Young, *A Sprig of Hope*. p. 27.

Original sin refers to the flaw in human nature that gives us all a bias towards evil — the sort of evil that could be described as the root selfishness that cuts us off from God and our fellow men.

David H. C. Read, *Overheard*, p. 74.

Adam and his son Abel were taking a walk some years after Adam and Eve had been expelled from Eden. They passed by that lovely garden, and Abel exclaimed: "Gee, Dad, what a beautiful place! Wouldn't it be nice to live there?" Adam paused a moment, then answered, "Well, son, we did live there one time, but your mother ate us out of house and home."

Skepticism

The old man is writing his autobiography. He begins it with words which my late Uncle Alex told me one time should be used by religious skeptics as a prelude to their nightly prayers. These are the words: "To whom it may concern!"
Kurt Vonnegut, *Slapstick,* p. 19.

Snob

I am a snob. I look down on people who look down on people.
Gert Behanna

Social Action

I do not see how any Christian with a "social conscience" intends to do without Christ; and I do not see how any disciple of His can fail to want the full blaze of His light to shine in every corner of our corporate life.
Sam Shoemaker

Here, as ordinarily before, the history of Judaism is best seen as a history of social behavior. This is no surprise to Jews, who have always made as much of Halakhah ("that by which one walks"), the binding rules, as of Haggadah, the narrative that expounds or interprets scripture.
Martin E. Marty, *A Nation of Behavers,* p. 63.

Solitude

But what about the problems in too much of too intense presence? One of the difficulties is in oneself — one has to preserve one's own center from the fatigue and dispersal that come from too many demands. Some solitude is necessary for any human being to preserve his capacity for presence. Solitude deepens and

clarifies it, while presence enriches and gives meaning to solitude.
Rollo May, *Paulus,* p. 31.

Sorrow

In *Romeo and Juliet,* Juliet's mother says to her after Tybalt's death: "Will you wash him from his grave with your tears?"

Sovereignty

I've not seen the play but the title speaks to me: *Your Arms Are Too Short to Box With God.* Of course they are. Who can do battle with God?

Status Quo

The seven worst words we can hear in a church: "We Never Did It That Way Before." They are especially dangerous when they are the seven last words.

Stewardship

"Dear Mr. Smith: In reply to your request to send a check, I wish to inform you that the present condition of my bank account makes it almost impossible. My shattered financial condition is due to the federal laws, state laws, county laws, corporate laws, mothers-in-law, sisters-in-law, and out-laws. Through these laws, I am compelled to pay a business tax, amusement tax, head tax, school tax, gas tax, light tax, water tax, and sales tax. Even my brains are taxed. I am required to get a business license, dog license, car license, truck license, not to mention a marriage license. I am also required to contribute to every organization or society which the genius of man is capable of bringing to life; women's relief, unemployment relief, every hospital and charitable institution in the city, including the Red Cross, the black cross, the purple cross and the double cross. For my own safety, I am required to carry life insurance, property insurance, liability insurance, tornado insurance, unemployment insurance, old age insurance and fire insurance. I am inspected, expected, disrespected, rejected, dejected, examined, re-examined, informed, reformed, summoned, fined, commanded, and compelled until I provide an inexhaustible supply of money for every known need, desire or hope of the human race. Simply because I refuse to donate something or other, I am boycotted, talked about, lied about, held up, held down, and robbed until I am ruined. I can tell you honestly that had not the unexpected happened, I could not enclose this check. The wolf that comes to so many doors now-a-days just had pups in the kitchen. I sold them." HERE IS THE MONEY!

THE MESSENGER -- Bethany United Methodist Church, Smyrna, GA, 1/26/76.

Strength

There's nothing as gentle as strength.
Robert Frost

Style

Fashions are always changing but the person with style is never out of date.
Baer's Almanac

I saw this in a novelty card shop: "I complained because I had no shoes until I saw a man who had no style."

Success

I've noticed it most always takes character and ability to become a success. But it takes more of both to live with success.

Suffering

I've discovered people are affected by the fire of suffering in basically one of two ways. They come out of it like bricks, hardened by the fire. Or they come out as gold does, purified and beautiful. Job said it, didn't he? "When he has tried me I shall come forth as gold." (Job 23:10)

Surrender

God can do wonders with a broken heart if you will give him

all the pieces.
Victor I. Alfsen

Symbolism

There is a story told of a woman who, on a trip to China, bought an old medallion which she liked so well she began to wear it almost constantly about her neck. Its bizarre and striking design always gave rise to interested conversation; and the woman became so fond of it she adopted it as her good-luck charm.

At a diplomatic dinner in Washington she met the Chinese ambassador who, she noticed, was observing the medallion with a faint smile upon his lips. "Have you seen one of these before, Ambassador?" the lady inquired. He admitted that he had and promptly changed the subject. "Would you be so kind as to translate the inscription on it?" the lady asked. The ambassador said that he would rather not. The lady insisted. "Very well, madam," he said at last with great reluctance. "It says 'Licensed Prostitute, City of Shanghai'. "

This little anecdote yields, as do most anecdotes, many instructive insights. For our present discussion it is illuminating in this respect: It illustrates the fact that unless we know the system of symbolism involved, a script can be directly in front of our eyes and we will remain in total ignorance of its meaning.

Gina Cerminara, *The World Within*, p. 45.

Tact

Tact is the unsaid part of what you say.

Talent

Use what talents you possess. The woods would be very silent if no birds sang there except the ones that sing best.
Henry Van Dyke

Teamwork

It ain't the individual
Nor the army as a whole

But the everlasting teamwork
Of every bloomin' soul.
J. Mason Knox

Temper

We must interpret a bad temper as the sign of an inferiority complex.
Alfred Adler

Temptation

Temptation is the devil looking through the keyhole. Yielding is opening the door and inviting him in.
Billy Sunday

Theology

The setting for doing theology is the covenant community. Our decisions and interpretations must be shared with the people of God and tested against their thought and experience. Theology is not a private affair.
Douglas E. Wingerer, *Beliefs,* p. 32.

Religion is an experience of God. Theology is merely an attempt to explain the experience.
Agnes Sanford, *Behold Your God,* p. 2.

Time

Consider our world. We're caught in a world of instant photos, fast foods, and permanent press clothes. We want a religion that zips along on the fast track. I can think of nothing wrong with conserving time, hurrying to get tasks done. But what do we do with the time we save?
Cecil Murphey, *Seven Daily Sins,* p. 33.

Time is the greatest of sponges; it sops up unpleasant memories as though they were sea water. Then you throw the sponge away and the bad memories have vanished.
Irving Stone, *The Greek Treasure,* p. 258.

Tolerance

Jesus had a purpose in mind when he criticized the disciples for discouraging those who cast out demons in his name, but who were not one of them. There is room for all and we should not readily turn from a true word of God because it is spoken by another person who does not walk with us.

Charles M. Laymon, *They Dared to Speak for God*, p. 19.

Trinity

God is more like a committee than a monarch. Possibly, the trinitarian formula is a fancy way of saying that just as God gave Adam a companion because it is not good for man to be alone, so he is revealing that it is not good for God to be alone either. The only true man is man-in-community because the only true God is God-in-community.

Colin Morris, *The Hammer of the Lord*, p. 154.

Trust

Trust is the increasing ability to live in a world I do not have to understand, that I do not have to control, that I do not have to order cognitively. Trust means getting on the other side of personality, getting on the other side of character.

Jim Fowler and Sam Keen, *Life Maps*, p. 114.

Through his way of saying this, and much more to similar purpose, he pleased himself on such confidential terms with me in an admirable manner; and I may state at once that he was always so zealous and honourable in fulfilling his compact with me that he made me zealous and honourable in fulfilling mine with him.

Charles Dickens, *Great Expectations*, p. 215.

Truth

Truth can come up all around you like a covey of quail into which you have walked; it will flutter its wings and pound and fly away.

Carlyle Marney

Every man seeks for truth, but only God knows who has found it.

Lord Chesterfield

Understanding

Smiley was around, but at the moment he could not have given Jerry any help at all. He would have traded all his knowledge for a little understanding.

John Le Carre, *The Honourable Schoolboy,* p. 497.

Unity

We are not one because men are not plugged into God. Consequently, there is no way we can get plugged into each other.

Tom Skinner, *Words of Revolution,* p. 26.

Vanity

Remember the queen in Snow White and the Seven Dwarfs? Every day she asks the magic mirror for reassurance, "Mirror, mirror on the wall, who is the fairest of them all?" It is inevitable that sooner or later when the queen goes to the mirror, she will learn that someone else in the kingdom is more beautiful than she. When that moment comes, tragedy will strike. Actually, though, the tragedy began for her long before, when she started asking the question. The queen, like so many of us, finds herself caught up in an obsession with eros, and eros characteristically fears time because it doesn't wear well. Because of its preoccupation with beauty and power, eros cannot endure time. People who have structured their lives around eros eventually discover the irreversibility of time. The foundations of eros slowly, relentlessly wear away, and as we come to a realization of what is happening to us, we may panic, or worse, like the queen, seek solutions that hurt those around us.

Earl F. Palmer, *Love Has Its Reasons,* p. 103.

Vision

I don't know who said it but I like it. "Those who hear not the music think the dancers mad."

Waiting

So the Bible extols waiting, partly because it requires qualities which the Lord wants to encourage in us, like patience, which I need so badly. But there is another reason too. Waiting works. It is a joining of man and God to achieve an end, and the end is always a form of the Easter story.

Catherine Marshall, *Adventures in Prayer*, p. 47.

War

Waste of muscle, waste of brain;
Waste of patience, waste of pain;
Waste of manhood, waste of health;
Waste of beauty, waste of wealth;
Waste of blood and waste of tears;
Waste of youth's most precious years;
Waste of ways the saints have trod;
Waste of glory, waste of God —
WAR!

James Armstrong, *Gentlemen . . . Start Your Engines*, p. 17.

Will

Because he died so soon after his separation from World-Wide, there was some talk that Fineman committed suicide, but the Hays office hushed it up so fast that it was impossible to track it down. Of course, there are less spectacular ways of taking your life than by gun or gas; there is the slow leak when the will is punctured, what the poet was trying to say when he spoke of dying of a broken heart.

Budd Schulberg, *What Makes Sammy Run?* p. 234.

Witness

Not merely in the words you say,
Not only in your deeds confess'd,
But in the most unconscious way
     Is Christ express'd.

For me 'twas not the truth you taught,
To you so clear, to me still dim;
But when you came you brought
    A sense of Him.

And from your eyes He beckons me,
And from your heart His love is shed,
'Till I lose sight of you — and see
    The Christ instead.
Author Unknown

When Lord Peterborough visited for a week with the great Fenelon, a famous preacher of the Middle Ages, he was so impressed with Fenelon's piety and service that he exclaimed when leaving, "If I stay here any longer, I shall become a Christian in spite of myself."

Every Christian is God's public-relations person.
Grace H. Churchill

Witnessing is evangelism that evangelizes the evangel and conversion that converts the converter.
E. Stanley Jones

Words

Stressing the value of a wide vocabulary, the instructor told the class, "Use a word ten times and it will be yours for life." In the back of the room a pert brunette looked out the window and chanted softly: "Tom, Tom, Tom, Tom, Tom, Tom, Tom, Tom, Tom, Tom."

Man does not live by words alone, despite the fact that sometimes he has to eat them.
Adlai Stevenson

Worry

In so many areas of life we exercise our minds on things we cannot affect.
Paul H. Beattie

Worship

Worship is the first priority of the church.
Wesley P. Ford

Worship is the interruption of work to celebrate.
Van Ogden Vogt

One day George McLeod, pastor of a church located on High Street in Glasgow, Scotland, chanced to look up at the stained glass windows over the chancel of the sanctuary. The phrase "Glory to God in the Highest" was carved in the glass. As he looked he noticed that a pane of glass was broken and missing, the pane on which the letter "e" in the word "highest" was carved. Suddenly he found himself seeing the words that were now there, "Glory to God in the High st." And it struck him that the only way to glorify God in the highest is to glorify him in the High St.

Perhaps it is because our building is located at the corner of Germantown Ave. and High St. that this story is so pertinent to our congregation. But perhaps it is pertinent to you and your congregation as well.

Robert A. Raines, *The Secular Congregation*, pp. 107-108.

Youth

Every street has two sides, the shady side and the sunny. When two men shake hands and part, mark which of the two takes the sunny side; he will be the younger of the two.
Bulwer-Lytton